TRANSCENDENTAL
DECEPTION

TRANSCENDENTAL
DECEPTION

Behind the TM curtain—bogus science, hidden agendas,
and David Lynch's campaign to push a million
public school kids into TRANSCENDENTAL MEDITATION
while falsely claiming it is not a religion.

ARYEH SIEGEL

Janreg Press   Los Angeles, California

Contact the author
info@tmdeception.com
tmdeception.com

Cover designed by
KrinskyDesign.com

ISBN 978-0-9996615-0-5

Library of Congress Control Number: 2017918475

Printed in the United States of America

First Printing: January, 2018

Dedicated to

Schwartzie

Contents

Author with Maharishi, Arosa Switzerland, August, 1974

Waking Up: Why I Wrote This Book and Why Now?

I learned Transcendental Meditation in 1971, and became a TM teacher in 1975. Working full-time for the national TM center, my wife and I both learned advanced TM techniques known as *siddhis* that were claimed to produce supernatural powers and enlightenment. To get there, I was meditating four hours a day as instructed. In 1981, ten years after I started TM, I concluded that it wasn't worth my time, and I quit.

While I was involved with TM, I had met its founder, Maharishi Mahesh Yogi, several times, and most of my friends were also TM teachers. Over time, I lost contact with all of them, and for almost thirty-five years I heard nothing about Transcendental Meditation. My life had moved on. I didn't even know that Maharishi had died until eight years after the fact.

Then in 2015, everything changed. Suddenly TM seemed to be everywhere. Film producer-director David Lynch had become the face of TM in the United States. His foundation was sponsoring high-profile fundraisers and educational conferences fueled by celebrity performances and attendees. They were promoting TM in public schools and the military (hoping to attract government funding for large-scale programs). Newspaper stories and magazine articles proclaimed TM to be the panacea for many of the world's problems, everything from calming troubled kids in school to curing PTSD in veterans. TM was even being presented as the solution to crime and as the highway to world peace. The majority of the articles were positive and unquestioning. Segments on news programs, such as *Good Morning America*, featured celebrity meditators and morphed into TM love fests. Oprah Winfrey paid for her employees to learn TM. Oprah even devoted segments of her television show to TM and traveled with her crew to film at TM's university in Fairfield, Iowa.

By this time, I had become a more observant Jew. Perhaps that's why I began noticing that every television or radio program promoting TM included a statement that TM was secular and had nothing at all to do with religion. This was often stated causally, almost as an afterthought. Regardless of how the line was delivered, I knew it wasn't true.

TM had become so mainstream that within a two-month period two of my friends and one of my business partners told me they were planning to learn it. So did my daughter-in-law. All of them were Jewish and observant. But why should that matter? After all, wasn't TM a scientifically validated mental technique that had absolutely nothing to do with religion?

They all knew that I had been a TM teacher, and each one of them asked me what I thought about TM. Without hesitation, I told them not to do it.

I knew from my training as a TM teacher that learning TM required participating in a Hindu religious ceremony, called a puja. As a teacher, I had to memorize the puja word for word in Sanskrit. It was performed in front of an altar with incense, chanting, and various offerings, and included bowing down to a photo of Maharishi's guru who was clad in orange robes. As far as I knew, the ceremony had not changed and most likely is still performed the same way as I had learned and performed it years ago.

When I was becoming a teacher, I was told that the puja preserved the purity of the TM teaching by thanking the great masters of the tradition who had passed it on throughout the millennia. And as crazy as it seems today, I didn't associate the puja at all with Hinduism. Maharishi had repeatedly said that TM was from the vedas, which was the root of all religions and each religion was a branch of the vedic tree. It would allow each branch to be appreciated and practiced more completely.

I didn't care much about any of this except as a TM marketing tool. I hardly knew anything about my own religion, let alone the vedas. I knew I wasn't becoming a Hindu, but I was confused. I was learning to perform a complex Hindu ritual that any sane observer would categorize as religious. But I didn't see it that way. I thought Maharishi was the holiest man on the planet, and I considered myself extremely fortunate that he was my guru. I was in a state of enchantment. I had turned off the logical thinking button in my brain. I bought whatever Maharishi said. If he said the puja wasn't religious, it wasn't religious. I think I believed it was just a thank you to Maharishi's teachers that happened to look religious. (Years later I would learn that the sounds in TM, known as "mantras," are the names of Hindu gods, even though the TM movement has always denied this.)

I've come to realize that saying TM is based in Hinduism, while true, is a disservice to the Hindu religion. Maharishi offered a simplified version of Hinduism that was actually rooted in guru worship, cobbled-together rituals, watered-down versions of classic Hindu beliefs, and exaggerated promises including super powers, perfect health, enlightenment, and eternal life. In the years after I left TM, Maharishi would slice and dice Hinduism like a corporate raider, selling anything he thought could make money. Today there are still many under his spell. They see TM as the one true way to enlightenment and higher consciousness. For them, TM is more important than anything else. As you'll learn in this book, that unquestioning belief has destroyed many lives. But the enchanted see no contradiction in worshipping someone who promised eternal life, even though he himself died. This kind of enchantment is rooted in the denial of critical thinking or doubt or questioning.

Some eighteen months ago, I read a biography of Rabbi Menachem Schneerson, one of the most important Jewish leaders of the twentieth century.[1] Remarkably, as early as 1961, Rabbi Schneerson recognized that meditation, if properly supervised, could be useful as an adjunct to medical and mental health treatment. He called for medical practitioners to be trained in a non-religious meditation that they could use as appropriate with their patients. However, by 1978, he was deeply concerned with the growth of cults and the large number of Jewish youth getting involved with them. In response, he wrote a confidential memorandum (and later spoke publicly) saying the rites and rituals associated with Transcendental Meditation and certain other meditation movements were rightly regarded by rabbinic authorities as cultic, bordering on (and in some respects actually being) idolatry. He wanted a meditation that would produce the benefits without any religious overlay. Not much happened. As it turned out, 1978 was the peak of my involvement in TM.

When my family and friends started to get caught up in TM's resurgence, what had up to that point been a casual observation became personal. Like the vast majority of people interested in TM, they wanted the benefits of meditation, not a new religion. As soon as I mentioned TM's hidden religiosity, they lost interest. I wondered, how many others were in the dark?

I decided to do some research. I thought I knew TM. However, within an hour of searching online, I was shocked to discover how remarkably weird TM had become. That initial hour turned into almost a year of research, interviews, and writing. What I found could be summarized in one word—deception. Very little about TM is what it seems. TM exists behind a curtain; much of it is hidden even from its biggest supporters. I came to understand that most everything TM does is calculated to market a variety of products—everything from TM instruction, advanced practices, various courses, to Maharishi branded elixirs, medicinals, and even skin care products. They also sell Hindu prayer services, vedic architecture, vedic organic vegetables, and astrology. You can even pay a million dollars to attend a special three-week course and become a leader in the TM organization. It's "pay to play" on steroids. Completing the course confers the title of a "raja," and you get to wear a little gold crown, a long white robe, and a beaded necklace. And this is only the tip of TM's fantasy world.

For all its celebrity and hype, TM has some very big problems.

First, it is based on, what I believe to be, Maharishi's perverted version of Hinduism. That is not a problem, per se, as the U.S. Constitution guarantees freedom of religion. My concern is that because religion in public schools is against the Constitution, to get into schools, TM must pretend it is a science and conceal its religious practices.

Another problem is that other meditation techniques produce similar, and often better, results than TM at a fraction of the cost. (TM currently charges $960 for its basic course.)

When I began my research, I knew nothing about mindfulness meditation. Mindfulness stems from the Buddhist tradition. I learned that the version known as Mindfulness Based Stress Reduction (MBSR) that was developed in the 1970s is secular. The Relaxation Response, to which I devote a chapter of this book, is essentially the TM technique without the TM mantra, Hindu trappings, or high cost. Both MBSR and the Relaxation Response provide therapeutic benefits without the religious overlay central to TM.

One thing you'll learn in this book is that meditation is not a cure-all. Both mindfulness and Relaxation Response advocates recognize that there are limitations to their benefits. And both realize that much more, and substantially higher quality research is necessary to define and refine what works best and for whom and in what situations. While everyone wants to be on the winning horse, both recognize that good science is as interested in learning what doesn't work as it is in what does.

Not TM. TM is promoted as the true and only way to inner transcendence, global peace, ending crime, and all the rest. It is the solution to every problem. I believe it is also an extreme form of grandiosity that sometimes borders on delusional thinking. I've realized this is based on nothing other than the Maharishi's dedication to self-promotion and self-glorification. The fact that many good, caring people believe TM is everything, is a testament to the seduction of Maharishi's storytelling abilities and their blind devotion to him.

TM proponents say that very few people have had any negative experiences practicing TM, and that those who did most likely had preexisting conditions that precipitated the problems they associated with TM. It wasn't difficult for me to find dozens of people who claim they were severely damaged by their TM practice. Some of them sued TM and the TM organization chose to pay large settlements rather than face them in court. I recount some of their stories in a chapter on TM casualties.

I thought I came out of TM unscathed. I hadn't thought about TM for decades. But in the process of writing this book, I discovered that I too was damaged. At some point I spoke with Don Krieger, one of the pioneers who created an online forum that exposed many of TM's highly guarded secrets. I wanted permission to include a story in the book that was personal to him. We spoke for a while and at one point he asked, "How did TM damage you?" I denied that it did and he didn't believe me. A few minutes after hanging up, I realized he was right. For the first time I began to confront the reality that despite two master's degrees and most of a Ph.D. from some top universities, I had not only turned off my critical thinking ability but I had also allowed myself to become infantilized. Not only did I drink Maharishi's Kool-Aid, I drank it by the gallon.

After reading extensively about cultic groups, attending workshops for cult survivors, and having discussions with cult experts like Steven Hassan and Patrick Ryan, I realized how insidious and damaging the experience had been. I became very concerned that TM's deceptions would continue to ensnare people looking to deal with stress into something that could prove very detrimental to some of them as it had to so many others and me over the years. Although sharing how I got caught up in TM is profoundly embarrassing, I realized there is no book currently out there that discusses TM's shadow side. So I decided to write the book. The chapters that follow are an exposé of Maharishi Mahesh Yogi and the organization he created. It provides information that school administrators, principals, and parents should have available to make an informed decision about TM in schools. I strongly believe it doesn't belong there. It gives celebrities information that may help them rethink if they want to continue promoting TM. And I invite journalists to apply critical thinking to the information presented by the TM organization and no longer accept that information at face value.

Introduction

So you decide to learn meditation. You've been hearing about meditation and mindfulness for years. Some friends and family members are now doing it. Sounds good. What could be simpler? You've read that meditation can reduce stress, improve concentration and productivity, and maybe even cure insomnia or high blood pressure. You are not interested in joining any religion, but you hear that meditation is not a religious practice and is based in scientific research. A co-worker raves about Transcendental Meditation. She's been doing TM for years and it has made a positive difference in her life. She talks about how so many celebrities do TM–from Oprah to Jerry Seinfeld. And it's so simple. You go through a short ceremony, get a special secret mantra, and then start quietly reciting your mantra for twenty minutes, twice a day. She assures you this is not a religion and the method has been scientifically validated. So you check it out and are surprised that it costs nearly a thousand dollars to receive this mantra, but you decide, What the Hell. Let's do it.

On the day of your introduction, you have been asked to bring two pieces of whole fruit, six fresh flowers, and a white handkerchief. You silence your phone, step through the front door, and quietly take off your shoes. As your instructor greets you, she places the items you've brought in a basket and tells you to make yourself comfortable on the sofa in the waiting area while she prepares the space where you will be learning Transcendental Meditation.

A few minutes later, she comes out and leads you back to a quiet, dimly lit room. It's small and cozy, furnished like the den of someone's house. The scent of incense fills your nose, and you can feel the soft plush carpet under your socks. There are two chairs in the center of the room, one for you and one for the teacher, and a small table with a framed picture of an old Indian man in orange robes. He looks like a guru, sitting in a lotus position that you are familiar with from your yoga class. You take another peek at the table. It looks like a small altar. You think to yourself, "What the hell is going on here? This looks a lot more religious than it does scientific." But you keep quiet. She starts by reminding you that she's chosen a personal mantra for you based on information you shared on your intake form. Because it is personal to you, you are not to share it with anybody: not your spouse, your parents, or even your children. If you forget your mantra, which is normal in the beginning, you can always set up a time to come see her at the center and she will remind you. She informs you that she will start meditating with you, and once you're in it, she will leave the room. She will come back a few minutes before the end of your twenty-minute session, so you don't need to worry about keeping track of time. You nod in agreement.

The fruit, flowers, and handkerchief you brought are laid out on the altar in front of the photo. Your instructor tells you that she is going to perform a ceremony thanking the teachers who have preserved this knowledge over the centuries, and that all you have to do is observe.

You listen as she sings several verses from memory in a language you don't understand. When she finishes, she motions for you to join her in bowing down towards the picture. You feel slightly awkward, but bow anyway, because you don't want to be rude or mess something up (or maybe you just want the full experience). As she slowly gets up, she whispers, almost imperceptibly, two syllables. Her voice gets louder as she gestures for you sit beside her and join her in repeating the sound. After about twenty seconds, her voice starts to get softer and softer. Eventually you notice, and you lower your own voice too, repeating the sound over and over until you are barely whispering. At this point she says, "When you're ready, simply keep repeating the sound gently in your head." So, you do.

At some point, you hear her leave the room. You realize you are practicing your first session of Transcendental Meditation.

Chapter 1

My Story

In the mid-1970s, I decided to become a TM teacher. My gradual immersion into the world of TM parallels that of many others. What started off as a casual interest to relieve stress, morphed into an all-encompassing way of life that lasted almost ten years.

I had a master's degree in Community Organization from the School of Social Welfare at Case-Western Reserve in Cleveland, and another from Berkeley in Public Health Planning. I had started practicing TM at the recommendation of my best friend at the time, a physician in the same graduate program at Berkeley.

After attending the required introductory lectures, I signed up to learn TM the following Saturday. The initial sessions presented how TM worked and described the mantras used to meditate as simple sounds that had no meaning. During the follow-up sessions, I had exposure to Maharishi and his teachings, but I recall only being told that practicing TM would lead to something called "cosmic consciousness." Supposedly, I would become enlightened for $35, which seemed a pretty good deal.

Initially, I was interested in the potential role of TM as an adjunct to traditional medicine. Eventually, my focus took a turn to the spiritual side, and I started exploring Eastern religions and philosophy. At the TM center, I watched videos of Maharishi discussing higher consciousness and presenting TM as the superhighway to enlightenment.

I attended weekend and week-long courses, and I was meditating significantly longer than twenty minutes, twice a day, as was recommended by the TM teachers who led these courses. Slowly but surely, I felt I was part of a movement. I had a guru who promised enlightenment, not only for me but also for the whole world.

When I took TM's teacher-training course in 1974 (a six-month requirement), I had the option of dividing the program into two segments. My first session in the summer was held at a hotel in Livigno, Italy, in the Alps. From what I recall, the routine entailed eight hours of daily meditation, each session lasting forty to fifty minutes. In between, we did a set of yogic postures (asanas) and five minutes of breathing exercises (pranayama). Evening videos featured Maharishi discussing how TM worked, higher consciousness, and his vision for a harmonious world that would automatically result if enough people meditated. (According to him, we were on the forefront of global transformation.)

Maharishi visited the course three times, each time staying for a few days. His first visit came when we were about two months into the three-month course. We expected he would come towards the end of the course. We were told this was a very rare surprise visit, and even though it was no longer a surprise, the excitement was palpable and the energy electric; this was quite a feat given how spaced out we were from all the meditation we had been doing.

Why all the excitement? The answer for me, why I was excited, is embarrassing even some forty plus years later. The words that best describe my state of mind are enchantment, enraptured, awe, and devotion. I had never been in the same room with someone that I considered "holy," let alone someone who was introduced everywhere as "his holiness." I had advanced degrees from outstanding universities and I turned off my critical thinking and analytical personality. I was "wow and bow" and devotion. It was emotionally overwhelming. The embarrassment is an appreciation of how I let myself become so infantilized.

There were probably a hundred of us in the course. Every one of us had interrupted our lives; most traveling long distances and paying a lot of money to somehow find our way to this hotel nestled in a small village in the Italian Alps, about a twenty-minute drive St. Moritz. We all had our own reasons for showing up. I came because I believed Maharishi offered a path to enlightenment. I had just come through a very rough divorce and enlightenment meant an end to the suffering I had been experiencing for a long time. I think at least a few others were in the same boat, leaving behind something better left in their personal rear view mirrors.

Another aspect of Maharishi's teachings appealed to that part of me that went into both social work and public health as career choices. My exploration of Eastern spiritual practices and teachings was interesting at first, but ultimately disappointing. I discovered that enlightenment was an individual path that involved finding a guru and basically detaching from the world. Maharishi, on the other hand, talked about higher consciousness ending suffering for everyone. Crime would be eliminated and lasting peace would come to the world. We, his missionaries, would spearhead this world transformation.

From the videos I watched before the course, I experienced Maharishi as clever, quick witted, and charming. He was certainly the most spiritual person I had ever encountered, and I had no doubt whatsoever that he was enlightened. I was counting the hours until he came.

Preparing for his visit, the staff scrubbed everything down and set up the meeting hall with chairs in a semicircle with a wide aisle separating them in the middle. I assumed Maharishi would walk down the middle aisle to the little stage with a seat that was set up for him. I made a plan to get a seat towards the front next to the middle aisle, which I did. The morning of the visit, bouquets of flowers surrounded his designated seat and a wonderful fragrance filled the room. A low table, covered with a white cloth, was placed in front of his seat and a microphone was set up on it.

I knew that when Maharishi entered a room, it was always a spectacle. He would slowly walk through adoring crowds, and those who could get close enough would present him with the most perfect rose they could buy. By the time he arrived at his seat, his arms were filled with roses, one of which he would often use as a prop when he spoke.

Our group planned to do the same. Everyone was rose-ready, but then another surprise. Instead of lining up to greet him with our flowers, we were going to be meditating as he walked in. The disappointment of missing the entrance procession would be tempered by Maharishi himself telling us to open our eyes. It seemed like a good trade, but it's not like we were given a choice. My seat choice was excellent—third row on the right aisle as he entered. Naturally, when I sensed he was coming in, I peeked. As he was passing my row, he slid off his wooden sandals, and that's where they stayed until he finished talking some hours later. I knew he would have to pause by my seat on the way out to slip on his sandals. My sense of abject embarrassment writing these words is tempered by the understanding I've gained as to the danger of surrendering one's critical thinking to a guru or messianic figure.

Fatefully, sneezing (of all things) got in the way of my fast track to enlightenment. The menu was vegetarian and always included full-fat yogurt, nuts, and whole-grain breads. As nutritious as it seemed, I was unaccustomed to that much dairy and wheat and started sneezing a great deal, and I was consistently congested. So, the breathing exercises never went well, and my meditations no doubt were affected. Thus, while the scenery was spectacular, the full experience eluded me. Nevertheless, I went to work for the movement.

Into the Movement

At some point, before I took the first three-month course to teach TM, I received an offer to direct TM's Institute for Social Rehabilitation. I can't remember the details of how the offer came about, but from what I could tell, the Institute existed in name only. (I would later learn this was a pattern that ran through the organization, at least at that point in time.) I would be responsible for organizing TM programs in rehabilitation settings, such as prisons, and substance abuse and mental health programs. I'd begin once I had completed the Italy course, and I would complete teacher training at some later point.

The Meaning of In

Following the course, I was invited to travel to Arosa, Switzerland, where Maharishi was based at the time. I was allowed to hang out with

Maharishi and the other "hanger-outers." The hotel that served as his headquarters was stunning. Open and spacious with large meeting rooms, it had a dining room stocked with an ample supply of yogurt, honey, and a variety of fresh fruit, nuts, and herbal teas. There were fresh flowers everywhere. I was housed in a small hotel a few blocks away, but only used it to shower and sleep because wherever Maharishi was, was the place to be.

There seemed to be a pecking order. At the top were the scientists that Maharishi kept around to create a veneer of scientific respectability. It seemed like they were all devotees.

Next were the "108's." They were elites who were allowed to hang around Maharishi, likely because they could afford to do so. Mostly in their mid-twenties and early-thirties, they dressed in Ivy League rich attire (casual and expensive) and, likely, many of their colleges were Ivy League as well. They attended to various tasks in support of the movement. Some of them were married, and I wondered if they were celibate. (I had heard rumors that Maharishi encouraged celibacy, even among married couples.) They covered all of their own expenses for hotels, meals, and travel. I assume they also made substantial donations in order to be in Maharishi's close circle.

The third group was the "Associate 108's." They had skills that were important to the movement, such as computer knowledge, printing, and graphic design. Their expenses were covered by the organization. If you didn't have the money to be in Maharishi's presence, having useful skills could get you there.

No one quite knew what to do with me, but since I was there, they must have assumed there must have been a good reason. I was left to myself and could go where I wanted. In addition to meditating, I spent several hours a day in the small audience when Maharishi was speaking or meeting visitors. I also took cable car rides up the mountains and went for long hikes. I stayed for three weeks. Just by virtue of being there, I was "in" and that felt like a big deal.

After arriving back in the U.S., there was some discussion as to where I would work. One possibility was at the recently acquired Maharishi International University (MIU) in Fairfield, Iowa. MIU originally

Our wedding October 1975, with Helen Lutes

Our wedding October 1975, with Helena "Mother" Olsen

launched in 1973, in an apartment complex in Goleta, California. In 1974, TM purchased the defunct Parsons College in Fairfield, Iowa and it was suggested that I consider locating there.

Open to the idea, I traveled to Fairfield to look around. I don't remember if I flew into Burlington or Cedar Rapids, but I do remember driving through long stretches of farmland. Fairfield was seemingly in the middle of nowhere. Arriving at the MIU campus, I found a dilapidated school on the outskirts of a small Iowa town that also seemed dilapidated. Walking around the campus was depressing. It looked like it had been unattended for years. Apparently, maintenance was low priority for Parsons once they decided to shut down. Within what felt like seconds, I had a rare moment of absolute clarity, and headed to the airport. There was no way I was moving to Fairfield.

Instead, I worked with some other TM teachers in a house we rented in Berkeley and started trying to identify possible government funding to test TM in rehabilitation programs. A few months later, I moved to Los Angeles to work at TM's national headquarters.

One of the first things I did at the office was to meet and thank Tova, the woman who made certain I was paid relatively on time. She always worked through my travel expense documentation, even though my receipts were a disaster. I wandered over to her office, and we spoke for about ten minutes before I asked her on a date. We were both recently divorced. She had a seven-year-old son and a five-year-old daughter. I also had a five-year-old daughter. We talked a lot about our kids on our first date. Eight months later, we were married.

The wedding was on a sunny, Sunday afternoon in October, in the backyard of the house Tova was renting at the time. Our TM-connected attendees outnumbered our relatives and other friends present. Most worked at the national or local TM center. TM royalty was also well represented. Helena Olsen (known as "Mother Olsen" because she and her husband hosted Maharishi in their home during his first trips to the U.S. and had remained close with him) cut our wedding cake. When things quieted down, she snuck off with Tova and me to perform a puja, or Hindu prayer. Helen and Charlie Lutes, who founded the Spiritual Regeneration Foundation in 1959 (the first TM organization in the U.S.) also attended. Other guests included David and Jessamine Verrill. They had been with Maharishi since 1959 or earlier, and both were also founders of the Spiritual Regeneration Movement.

Fundraising for the Cause

My work for the organization included continued attempts to get government grants to fund TM programs in rehabilitation settings and encourage research to track results. I also gave presentations on TM as an adjunct to rehabilitation treatments at various national and regional conferences. One of the main problems was getting government agencies to pay for TM instruction. It was a major stumbling block, and Maharishi refused to waive the initiation fees. I thought it was extremely shortsighted, and it hindered my work. While it was relatively easy to get agreement to do a study, it was very difficult to get government funding to pay for TM instruction.

However, one study that I co-authored with Allan Abrams was a success. George Ellis, a TM teacher, had started a TM program at Folsom State Prison. Allan and I designed the study and went to the prison to review the parameters with George. We were also curious to see how many inmates showed up to meditate. We both thought George was exaggerating the numbers. He wasn't.

Folsom was one of the toughest prisons in the country. Walking into the prison past security remains one of the scariest experiences of my life. George led us to a huge, open area designated for the meditation class. Within that extremely noisy open space, which had several other prisoner activities going on, was a "classroom." As I remember it, the classroom was basically four walls made of four-foot-high partitions and no ceiling. Allen and I both thought George was putting us on. We waited nervously as prisoners entered at the designated class time, convinced the location could not work.

Amazingly, when the meditation began, you could hear a pin drop—not only in the small, makeshift classroom, but also in the entire surrounding area. George had introduced me to one of the inmate meditation leaders, Sonny Barger. What he didn't tell me was that Sonny was the president of the Hell's Angels. When I commented on the unbelievable quiet, George told me who Sonny was and said, "Do you think anyone here is going to disturb Sonny's meditation?"

Our study was the lead article in the March 1978 issue of the journal *Criminal Justice and Behavior*.[1] Instant status!

The Times, They Are a-Changin'

In the 1970s, Merv Griffin hosted a popular television talk show. In 1975, my family and I attended both tapings of the *Merv Griffin Show* when Maharishi was the featured guest. He was the solo guest on the first show. The second time, he shared the spotlight with Clint Eastwood, who had recently learned TM.

TM credited the 1975 *Merv Griffin Show* appearances with attracting nearly 300,000 new initiates, including celebrities and New Age figures. TM teachers also appeared on more university campuses, and Maharishi's books were selling well. One, *The Science of Being and Art of Living*, was a disjointed explanation of the theory behind TM. Another provided commentary on the first six chapters of the Hindu scripture, the *Bhagavad Gita*. Those were heady times in my life, but TM was about to change.

Selling Superman and Wonder Woman

The enormous wave of initiations after the *Merv Griffin Show* appearances was similar to the interest sparked years earlier when The Beatles followed Maharishi to India. But within two years, interest dropped and the number of new initiates plummeted. Perhaps motivated by a diminished cash flow, Maharishi created the siddhi program. One common definition of a siddhi is a miraculous power imparted by the late stages of intense meditation.[2] Maharishi promoted the siddhis as a dramatic accelerant to enlightenment; he also promised the *siddha* (one practicing the siddhis) superhuman powers: levitation, invisibility at will, super-vision, super-hearing, the strength of an elephant, and omniscience. Yes, you read that list correctly, it includes omniscience. Perhaps as a bonus, Maharishi tossed in "eternal life." Cost for the course ranged from three thousand to ten thousand dollars; an enormous amount of money in the late '70s, especially for underpaid TM teachers. However, as full-time employees of the national center, Tova and I didn't have to pay.

Becoming Enlightened—Or Not

Once instructed, we followed the siddha directions faithfully. We even paid a monthly fee to participate in group siddha meditations in a foam-lined warehouse in West Los Angeles. Although I devoted well over four hours a day to TM and the siddhis for well over a year, I did not experience anything Maharishi promised. Nor, from what I could tell, did anyone else. What was called levitation was a total joke. While most people think of levitation as hovering in mid-air, in the TM world it consisted of mostly younger, more athletic siddhas hopping around on their butts on thick, dense foam pretending they were flying through the air. Maharishi had to do some fancy footwork to explain the absurdity of what was happening. In the process, he brilliantly redefined what normal, everyday people meant by levitation. He said the hopping was the "first stage" of levitation and called it "yogic flying." (This first stage has now lasted well over forty years.) Based on my total lack of results, I was happy that my course was free.

I also recognized that other aspects of TM were failing me. Importantly, my strong research background led to a troubling realization: nearly every study done by TM researchers was at least somewhat biased, and most were poorly designed. To be fair, I had to include the study that I co-authored at Folsom Prison in that assessment.

At that point, I stood at a career crossroads.

I thought that strengthening my skills in research design and analysis would make me a more valuable resource if the movement was interested in higher quality studies. If not, I could move on with a marketable skill set. In 1977, I was accepted into a Ph.D. program in behavioral science research in the UCLA School of Public Health. By that September, I was a full-time student, working full-time in my TM position, and doing my TM and siddha program four hours a day. Also, we had a new baby daughter.

My life was complicated, but it was about to become much simpler. For reasons that remain unclear to me to this day, TM's hierarchy changed dramatically. Without any explanation, Jerry Jarvis, who ran TM in the U.S., disappeared from the national center. Next to Maharishi, he was the most beloved person in TM. I can't remember what we thought had happened to him; I only remember feeling uncomfortable that he was there one day and gone the next, with no explanation. Then, the office was reorganized. Within a few weeks, my wife and I, along with almost everyone else, were told to leave.

We continued to meditate, and our programs continued to average about two hours in the morning and two in the evening. I'd like to say I remember the time "flying" by, but it didn't. The program was highly structured. It included thirty to forty minutes of TM, repetition of the nineteen English phrases (*sutras*) that comprised the various siddhis we were given, breathing techniques (*pranayama*), yogic postures (*asanas*), and rest periods. Every session was capped off with reading about Hindu gods who are fighting malignant demons in a Hindu scripture known as the ninth mandala of the rig veda.

Eventually, we stopped going to the group "flying" program. We put foam mattress pads in our garage and did our program at home. It gave us more flexibility and cut down travel time to and from the meditation warehouse, along with saving the monthly fee. Some months later, a woman who identified herself as from the TM national office called to inform us that we were no longer welcome at the group meditation center and that our admission badges had to be returned. When I asked why, she said we had "disowned the movement." We didn't care, because we had moved on with our lives. Still, it was strange as we had never said anything negative about Maharishi or the TM organization.

Fast Forward to Today

Within a year of getting booted from our jobs, Tova and I stopped meditating. Our lives were filled with family and work, and the goings-on of daily life. We had two more children. I ran a community mental health center for several years and then worked as a planner in a large Jewish Federation. After nine years, I left the Federation to become a commercial real estate broker (which I continue to do to this day). Tova finished her B.A. degree and then trained as a certified nurse midwife at the University of Southern California Medical School. There, she delivered babies for five years and held a faculty appointment in the medical school. Then, after delivering hundreds of babies at LAC+USC Women's Hospital, she left and started a home birth practice. Finally, tired of always being on call, she stopped deliveries and spent the next fifteen years doing gynecology in a woman's health center. She recently retired but continues to deliver most of our grandchildren and great-grandchildren.

TM faded into the distant past until 2015, when I noticed a steady parade of well-publicized, glowing endorsements of TM by various celebrities. I couldn't help myself. I got curious about this most recent revival and visited TM.org, the organization's flagship website for the U.S. market. I found more of the same: celebrities extolling the benefits of TM, and claims of TM's positive effect on a host of medical and mental health issues.

I learned that David Lynch had become the chief promoter of TM in the U.S. I didn't know who David Lynch was, but he was clearly primarily responsible for the wave of celebrity endorsements. In addition to large-scale conferences and fundraisers targeting educators and the military, in the spring of 2017, the David Lynch Foundation held a sold-out fundraiser at the Kennedy Center in Washington, D.C. Hugh Jackman hosted the evening, with entertainment provided by Jerry Seinfeld and Jay Leno. Musical acts by Ke$ha and others added more star power.

But where was Maharishi? The man who introduced TM to the world over sixty years ago and controlled the organization with an iron grip until his death in 2008, barely had a presence on the TM.org website. Aside from a thumbnail photo relegated to the top-left corner of the site, Maharishi was missing in action.

Tova and I became TM teachers in the pursuit of higher consciousness. Higher consciousness was all Maharishi talked about in our teacher training courses and the video discourses we watched for hours on end. Today, there's not even a hint of "higher consciousness" on TM.org. There's no mention of the TM-Sidhi techniques that take between four to six hours a day to perform, and that Maharishi promised would accelerate enlightenment and grant us the power to levitate, along with a *holy* host of other supernatural powers, including omniscience and eternal life. We, his faithful teachers, would do our part to end crime, create world peace, make nations invincible, and bring heaven down to earth. I wondered—how had Maharishi's lofty promises of enlightenment been reduced to such mundanities as lower blood pressure and better sleep?

I did some more digging and found that the price of instruction had dropped from $2,500 at the time he died, to just under $1,000 in recent years. Still a high price for meditation, but an alarming decline nevertheless. One explanation makes the most sense: the organization is struggling to recruit new initiates. That would explain the PR push. But why was Maharishi downplayed? Why was higher consciousness absent from the pitch? The answer I found was that TM is, once again, courting government funding.

A major goal of the David Lynch Foundation is to expand teaching TM in public schools. A major goal of this book is to prevent that from happening. Beyond teaching kids to relax, the TM organization and the David Lynch Foundation want the public to believe TM is a cure for post-traumatic stress disorder, autism, hyperactivity, drug abuse, and even homelessness. And, they want government funding to pay for TM instruction. Taxpayer-funded programs offer tremendous income potential for the TM organization. However, to gain acceptance in public schools, TM has to steer clear of the First Amendment's Establishment Clause of the U.S. Constitution separating church and state. To do so, it has to keep secret its cosmic goals and pose as a secular, scientific, relaxation technique. It has to seem as American as apple pie.

Aryeh Siegel

Chapter 2

Behind the Veil

When you learn TM, are you participating in a religious ritual? Is it religious even if you don't intend for it to be? Does it matter? Does the answer differ if you are told that your experience is not religious?

The first deception people encounter when they come into contact with TM is being told it is not a religion. Most people walking through the doors of TM centers aren't looking for a new religion or a spiritual practice. I certainly wasn't. I wanted to learn how to meditate because I thought it would help me manage the stresses in my life. However, if I had known that I would be participating in Hindu rituals and had understood the meaning of the Sanskrit verses my instructor would be chanting, it's quite possible that I would have walked away. Every single person who has learned Transcendental Meditation over the last fifty years has participated in the exact same initiation ceremony. And likely, not one of them was told by their TM teacher that what they were doing was in any way religious. That's because its founder, Maharishi Mahesh Yogi, designed it that way.

The second deception people encounter when starting TM is being told that TM mantras have no meaning. The fact is that they are the names of Hindu deities. They have no meaning to people learning TM because their teachers withhold the meaning. TM is rooted in

Hinduism—a Hinduism that Maharishi exploited and twisted to suit his personal and financial ambitions.

The question is, why? The answer is simple. Maharishi's major contribution to meditation was not the secretive initiation procedure or the mantras, but rather the technique itself: the relaxed, non-focused, self-paced repetition of a sound. Before TM, the majority (although not all) of meditation techniques involved some sort of concentration. Maharishi emphasized a non-concentrative meditation practice, while most other approaches didn't. However, he oversimplified it and tried to use the issue to unfairly discredit other approaches.

What Maharishi really did to revolutionize meditation was mass-market his non-concentrative technique. Even according to Maharishi, the mantra or word used didn't actually matter.[1] This is important to note because, if the sound doesn't matter, there is no reason to pay large amounts of money for a "unique" TM mantra when you can learn the technique from a book. Obscuring this fact, and many others, allowed Maharishi to build an empire.

The Puja

The puja is an ancient Hindu ritual or ceremonial worship service, one purpose of which is to create a channel of transmission from a divine object of worship to the one performing the puja ceremony. Objects of worship can be various Hindu deities or gurus who are believed to embody the divine. While Maharishi seems to have made his up, there are many variations of pujas, but they all essentially have the same function.

In the puja, offerings are made to the object of devotion, often represented by a painting or an idol, to earn his love and blessings. The offerings—usually fruit, candles, incense, flowers—symbolize surrendering one's mind, body, thoughts, desires, actions, and possessions to divine beings or gurus and enjoying whatever may come back as a gift from them. The deity or guru whose image is worshipped in the puja is considered a living incarnation of the deity. They are treated as if the deity has descended from above and actually inhabits the image.[2]

At this point, a fair question might be, "What can this possibly have to do with Transcendental Meditation which is a scientific, completely secular relaxation technique?"

Surely, no public school would allow its students to participate in a Hindu religious practice, just as they wouldn't allow them to participate in a Christian, Jewish, or Muslim religious practice. Certainly, those responsible would not encourage students to participate in a religious practice that likely conflicts with the students' own religion, especially when doing so in a public school violates the United States Constitution. Certainly, they would have thoroughly vetted TM before using public funds to pay for TM instruction or even accepting donations from outside organizations such as the David Lynch Foundation that raises money to pay for TM instruction in various settings, including public schools.

One would expect school administrators who allowed TM in their schools to have done all of these things, but apparently they didn't. Full-time TM instructors oversee the TM program in schools. Many classroom teachers along with the school principal and other school staff likely practice TM because they are offered free instruction.[3] TM teachers tell them that TM is not a religion because you don't have to believe in anything to do TM. It is a testament to TM's marketing that so many people go along with TM's "not a religion" hype after experiencing the puja, which both looks and feels religious. However, those entrusted with the care of our children must be held to a higher standard. When they experienced the puja, they should have immediately known that TM didn't belong in public schools.

Maharishi was, without doubt, one of the wealthiest gurus in history. His estate was reportedly in the billions when he died.[4] As fixated on money as he was, I have no doubt that he would have dumped the puja if he could have, because more people would have learned TM and, more importantly, the door to large-scale government funding would have been more open. But Maharishi couldn't get rid of the puja because it is the very heart of TM.

In fact, nothing about the puja is subject to change. Nothing can be changed because it is all considered holy and sacred. This includes the name "puja," all aspects of the ritual offerings, and the precision of their performance along with the Sanskrit chanting—all are absolute.

As described later in this chapter, Maharishi believed the puja, along with his mantras, invited the influence of Hindu deities into the lives of those doing TM. Maharishi also believed that his mantras were powered by a mystical connection to the guru and deities created during the puja. This highly guarded secret is evidenced by minutes of a meeting dated February 6, 2007, conducted by TM's "Raja of Atlanta," or head administrator at the time, Rogers Badgett. Speaking to the local directors, Badgett begins with a story about Arjuna, a central figure in Hindu scripture and considered the greatest archer and warrior of his time:

> The great general was teaching Arjuna about all the celestial weapons and how to use them. After the training, Arjuna tried to use them. They wouldn't work. The great general told him, "There has to be dakshina for them to work." **Dakshina is a gift, like the fruit, flowers and course fee to learn TM. For our own understanding, the technique isn't going to work until there is dakshina. We don't tell the general public this**. (Bold added.)[5]

So, no matter if you are a private person, a ten-year-old public school student, a captain of industry, or a celebrity, when you learn TM, the puja is non-negotiable.

There is a booklet known in TM as "The Holy Tradition" that pays homage to the gods and gurus who Maharishi claimed preserved the teaching of TM over the millennia. When TM became "scientific," "The Holy Tradition" was problematic for TM's new scientific image, and hard copies are difficult to come by. However, "The Holy Tradition" is available online, and following are some direct quotes describing the desired mental state of the TM teacher during the puja taken from "The Holy Tradition."

"Having recited this and having filled our minds and hearts with the meaning of what we say, we complete the invocation to the long tradition of the great masters and feel the inspiration of their glory. With heart thus secure in deep devotion, and mind upheld in the meaning of the recitation, our hands and eyes engage in the act of offering."

"The invocation through the offering is symbolic of our universal behavior towards invited and honored guests. Naturally we offer them the best we have in the house flowers, fruit, light, bath, shower, towels, good food. We greet them with loving reverence and sweet words. The ceremony of offerings has similar significance in that it expresses gratitude on a physical level and everything is done in a very natural, innocent and spontaneous manner."

"It may be that someone, seeing us making offerings before a picture, might argue that we are a sect and label us as such, and thereby try to depreciate the universality of the Spiritual Regeneration Movement [The first TM corporation in the US]. Nevertheless, these formalities, this style of offering, are ways of bowing to GURU DEV or expressing our reverence to the Holy Tradition."[6]

When Maharishi understood early on that the puja would turn many Westerners off, he trained his TM teachers to use deceptive language in order to hide the puja's centrality to TM. He also coached them to downplay the fact that those learning TM play an active role in the puja by bringing several items that are offered on the altar and being invited to join with the TM instructor in bowing down to the picture of Maharishi's teacher at the conclusion of the ritual. And this deception continues in full force today.

The Puja Prayer

The puja is chanted in Sanskrit, an ancient Indian language used primarily for religious purposes. The Hindu scriptures, the Vedas, are written in Sanskrit. The Sanskrit words are believed to have special vibrational power when recited in the context of the puja, in front of the image of the divine guru, as offerings are made. This is clearly a religious practice. But unless someone learning TM understands Sanskrit, he or she will have no idea what the TM teacher is chanting.

The TM organization won't give out translations of the puja to anyone—not to people who want to learn TM, not to school administrators or teachers, not to parents, not to the media.

The TM organization does not want anyone to know what the puja says or means. Even if you pay nearly a thousand dollars for your mantra, TM won't give you the text of your ceremony. They deliberately keep people in the dark. How bizarre is that? How scientific?

Too many years have passed for me to remember how we were taught the puja. In 1977, the TM organization was a defendant in a case that challenged TM being taught in New Jersey's public schools. The court transcript provides a wealth of information about many aspects of TM, including how TM teachers learned the puja. The court said prospective TM teachers were given the puja with Sanskrit written phonetically in English.[7]

Below is an English translation of the puja supplied by TM to the New Jersey court. Those familiar with the Hindu religion will recognize well-known Hindu gods and gurus. They will also know that gurus play an important role in Hinduism. In fact, some gurus are worshiped as divine beings.

INVOCATION

Whether pure or impure, whether purity or impurity is permeating everywhere, whoever opens himself to the expanded vision of unbounded awareness gains inner and outer purity.

INVOCATION

To LORD NARAYANA, to lotus-born BRAHMA the Creator, to VASHISHTHA to SHAKTI and his son, PARASHAR. To VYASA, to SHUKADEVA, to the great GAUDAPADA, to GOVINDA, ruler among the yogis, to his disciple, SHRI SHANKARACHARYA, to his disciples PADMA-PADA and HASTA-MALAKA,

And TROTAKACHARYA and VARTIKA-KARA, to others, to the tradition of our Masters, I bow down.

To the abode of the wisdom of the SHRUTIS, SMRITIS and PURANAS, to the abode of kindness, to the personified glory of the LORD, to SHANKARA, emancipator of the world, I bow down.

To SHANKARACHARYA, the redeemer, hailed as KRISH-NA and BADARAYANA, to the commentator of the BRAHMA SUTRAS, I bow down.

To the glory of the Lord I bow down again and again, at whose door the whole galaxy of gods pray for perfection day and night.

Adorned with immeasurable glory, preceptor of the whole world, having bowed down to Him we gain fulfillment.

Skilled in dispelling the cloud of ignorance of the people, the gentle emancipator, BRAHMANANDA SARASVATI, the supreme teacher, full of brilliance, Him I bring to my awareness.

Offering the invocation to the lotus feet of SHRI GURU DEV, I bow down.

Offering a seat to the lotus feet of SHRI GURU DEV, I bow down.

Offering an ablution to the lotus feet of SHRI GURU DEV, I bow down.

Offering cloth to the lotus feet of SHRI GURU DEV, I bow down.

Offering sandal paste to the lotus feet of SHRI GURU DEV, I bow down.

Offering full rice to the lotus feet of SHRI GURU DEV, I bow down.

Offering a flower to the lotus feet of SHRI GURU DEV, I bow down.

Offering incense to the lotus feet of SHRI GURU DEV, I

bow down.

Offering light to the lotus feet of SHRI GURU DEV, I bow down.

Offering water to the lotus feet of SHRI GURU DEV, I bow down.

Offering fruit to the lotus feet of SHRI GURU DEV, I bow down.

Offering water to the lotus feet of SHRI GURU DEV, I bow down.

Offering a betel leaf to the lotus feet of SHRI GURU DEV, I bow down.

Offering a coconut to the lotus feet of SHRI GURU DEV, I bow down.

Offering camphor light white as camphor, kindness incarnate, the essence of creation garlanded with BRAHMAN, ever dwelling in the lotus of my heart, the creative impulse of cosmic life, to That, in the form of GURU DEV, I bow down.

Offering light to the lotus feet of SHRI GURU DEV, I bow down.

Offering water to the lotus feet of SHRI GURU DEV, I bow down.

Offerings handful of flowers GURU in the glory of BRAHMA, GURU in the glory of VISHNU, GURU in the glory of the great LORD SHIVA, GURU in the glory of the personified transcendental fullness of BRAHMAN, to Him, to SHRI GURU DEV adorned with glory, I bow down.

The Unbounded, like the endless canopy of the sky, the omnipresent in all creation, by whom the sign of That has been revealed, to Him, to SHRI GURU DEV, I bow down.

GURU DEV, SHRI BRAHMANANDA, bliss of the Absolute, transcendental joy, the Self-Sufficient, the embodiment of pure knowledge which is beyond and above the universe like the sky, the aim of "Thou art That" and other such expressions which unfold eternal truth, the One, the Eternal, the Pure, the Immoveable, the Witness of all intellects, whose status transcends thought, the Transcendent along with the three gunas, the true preceptor, to SHRI GURU DEV, I bow down.

The blinding darkness of ignorance has been removed by applying the balm of knowledge. The eye of knowledge has been opened by Him and therefore, to Him, to SHRI GURU DEV, I bow down. Offering a handful of flowers to the lotus feet of SHRI GURU DEV, I bow down.[8]

TM promotes itself as being secular and scientific.

Does any of this sound secular and scientific?

In addition to memorizing the words, the teachers were also required to memorize the melody to which the puja is chanted, as well as the gestures and hand movements used during the chant. In earlier courses, would-be teachers had to perform the chant in front of, and to the satisfaction of, Maharishi. In my course in 1975, while Maharishi personally gave us our mantras, one of the course leaders tested us on the puja.

The court transcript documents the movements made by the teacher during the puja; the teacher makes fifteen offerings to Guru Dev and fourteen obeisances to Guru Dev. An obeisance is a movement of the body made as a token of respect or submission to the object of worship. The initial fourteen obeisances are then followed by three additional offerings and three more obeisances.

Finally, the puja ends with a string of divine epithets that are applied to Guru Dev. Guru Dev is called "The Unbounded," "the omnipresent in all creation," "bliss of the Absolute," "transcendental joy," "the Self-Sufficient," "the embodiment of pure knowledge which is beyond and above the universe like the sky," "the One," "the Eternal," "the Pure," "the Immovable," "the Witness of all intellects, whose status transcends thought," "the Transcendent along with the three gunas," and "the true preceptor."

The Court is very clear: "No one would apply all these epithets to a human being."

In case anyone has any lingering doubts that TM is a religion, the transcript of the New Jersey court decision will put those doubts to rest.

In describing the initiation process that applies to everyone who has ever learned TM, the court stated that each TM student was asked to bring a clean white handkerchief, a few flowers, and three or four pieces of fruit to the puja. (Former friends who became teachers in the early 1970s said that Maharishi didn't hide the symbolism of these offerings on their courses: the white cloth symbolizes the offering of the soul of the initiate; the flower signifies the blossoming of the Lord's presence in the initiate's heart; the fruit represents all the fruits of future actions, i.e. material wealth, success, happiness, and so forth.)

The transcript continued that upon arrival, the handkerchief, flowers, and fruit were placed in a container, and the TM student was led to a small room and asked to remove his or her shoes before entering the room. Inside the room was a rectangular table covered by a white sheet that served as an altar. The altar held a brass candleholder and a brass incense holder containing a candle and incense, both of which were lit by the teacher. The altar also held three brass dishes containing water, rice, and sandal paste. There was also a small brass dish containing camphor. Also, there is a tray on the table and an eight-by-twelve-inch color picture of Guru Dev at the back of the table. By 1977, Guru Dev had already been dead for over twenty years.

(How weird is it that TM pretends it is scientific and secular when learning TM requires making offerings on an altar to a long-dead guru?)

The court noted that a week or two before the puja, each student was required to sign a document promising never to reveal his or her mantra; they weren't given a copy of the document. The court also noted that the students were told that the puja was not a religious exercise or prayer. How is it possible that a public school official who had experienced the puja could think this was appropriate for school children? How could they not challenge any TM teacher who told them the puja wasn't religious?

It is almost incomprehensible that TM has been able to get away with this intentional deception for over fifty years. Repeating over and over again that TM is a science and is secular has fooled many very intelligent, caring, and well-meaning people, but that doesn't mean that its very core is not a Hindu religious practice.

To be very clear, I have no issue with the Hindu religion. My only issue is with deception.

Consider walking into a Catholic church or a Jewish synagogue for the first time to pray. The service may seem strange to someone unfamiliar with it. However, the prayer books are in a language you understand, and if you have questions, the Priest or Rabbi will answer them; there are no secrets. Nothing is withheld or hidden. Every word is there to see.

While mindfulness meditation originated in the Buddhist tradition, a completely secular version has been available since the 1970s. If someone wants to join the millions of people who practice mindfulness meditation, there are dozens, if not hundreds, of free courses on the Internet, scores of DVDs and CDs, and hundreds of smartphone apps that are free or low cost. Dozens of mindfulness instruction books are available for ten to twenty dollars, and seminars and various weekend or longer courses are frequently available.

Similarly, if someone wants to learn the Relaxation Response, there are many books, DVDs, and CDs available. Books by Dr. Herbert Benson that provide complete "how to" instructions have sold millions of copies. Interestingly, the method used to trigger the Relaxation Response is almost identical to the TM technique, except individuals choose the sound they use during the meditation instead of being assigned a secret mantra.

How has TM been able to get away with the science pretense for so long? How has it been possible to get away with fooling otherwise intelligent people? I believe part of the answer is that most people simply don't expect someone to lie to them. And that is what Maharishi did. He trained his teachers to never reveal the truth about what's going on.

I did a little experiment. I recently spoke with two TM teachers in Los Angeles, and a third teacher at TM's university in Fairfield, Iowa. I told all three that I was interested in starting TM, but before doing so, I wanted to get an English translation of the puja ceremony. I asked, "Could I get the translation of the ceremony before starting TM?" I was looking for a simple "yes" or "no" answer. It seemed a reasonable request, especially given that I was being asked to pay almost a thousand

41

dollars to learn TM.

The answers below are quotes from the TM teachers interviewed and taken from my contemporaneous notes of those conversations. All three said, "The puja maintains the purity of the TM teaching, so it can't change." Another said, "I'm just a regular American person, so I don't teach in my name, but in the name of a holy tradition. The ceremony aligns me with those great masters who have gone before me, and I symbolically create a sense of gratitude to them that enlivens TM for the student."

That was actually the closest anyone got to what TM teachers believe they are doing in the puja. He recognized his role as a conduit, and he said the puja enlivens TM for the student. Regardless, he was describing religion. A "holy tradition" is hardly a scientific term.

Another TM teacher stated, "The teacher just recalls the names of the most prominent leaders in the past and the ceremony is just part of a beautiful tradition that's not watered down or modernized." (Deities and gurus are conveniently redefined as leaders). He also said, "It's 99.9% for the teacher. The teacher brings most of the things used in the ceremony. The student brings a few things like some flowers and fruit and just witnesses the teacher performing the ceremony." He also said, "The teacher is thinking about the meaning so the student doesn't have to and that makes the transmission as pure as possible for the student."

One might ask, just who is making the transmission and how is it being made? If this is science, it is a very mystical version.

Two of the TM teachers said, "It's just like in karate when two opponents bow to each other out of respect before a match." That must be a favorite. I had previously heard it from one of the full-time TM teachers in the San Francisco public schools. (He also said, "We just tell them it's a song.") One answered, "I don't have anything written down. It's all memorized." And another said, "The teachers don't have the translation." I think my favorite answer was, "That's a great question. I don't know if anyone has ever asked it before." He also was reassuring, "It does have an Eastern flavor that many people find sweet or they are neutral. Worst case, it only takes a few minutes and you only have to do it once."

I repeatedly pushed for an answer. Could I get a written translation of the text of the puja? Yes or No? While two of the teachers said they didn't have the translation, the third one told me to come to the lectures at my local TM center. When I was ready to start TM, there would be an opportunity to bring up any personal issues with my local TM teacher privately. I knew it was a diversion. I knew that I would never be given the translation. Forty-two years since I started TM, and the deceit continues unchecked.

If TM acknowledged the simple truth, they wouldn't be able to sell their wares to public schools, to corporations, or to institutions. As will be documented throughout this book, TM's true believers must engage in endless deceptions and rationalizations to achieve their goals. Given honest information, the vast majority of people are quite capable of making appropriate decisions that impact their life. TM's true believers conceal the very information anyone should have before making a decision to start TM. And if regular people deserve honest information, how much more important is that information to those with significant responsibility for our children's well-being.

The Mantra

Beacon Light of the Himalayas is a booklet described as a "souvenir" of a meeting that took place in Kerala, India, in 1955. The book presents a straightforward transcription of talks given by Maharishi and others over several days to an Indian audience. In Maharishi's words, the Hindu religious assembly was primarily organized to pay homage to Maharishi's teacher, Guru Dev, or Divine Teacher. The event took place two years before Maharishi first traveled to the West, before he realized he would have to recalibrate his message to sell TM to a Western audience.

Maharishi spoke in English. No one, therefore, can claim that the intended meaning of his words was misinterpreted. The manuscript exposes several inconvenient truths about Maharishi and TM.

FLAG HOISTING

THE DAWN OF A HAPPY NEW ERA

IN THE FIELD OF SPIRITUAL PRACTICES

MIND CONTROL, PEACE

&

ATMANANDA

Through simple & easy methods of Spiritual Sadhana

propounded

by

Maharshi Bala Brahmachari Mahesh Yogi Maharaj

OF

UTTAR KASI, HIMALAYAS.

SOUVENIR OF THE GREAT SPIRITUAL DEVELOPMENT CONFERENCE OF KERALA., OCTOBER, 1955.

The Secret Meaning of Mantras

Most people are familiar with the word "mantra." Today, the term commonly refers to a popular word or slogan (e.g., "don't worry, be happy"). The original Hindu-Buddhist meaning mainly describes a word or sound that helps quiet the mind. Along those lines, the fundamental process of meditating uses one of the senses to focus on something, such as a sound, one's breath, or a candle flame that allows the mind to experience whatever that element is in ever more refined or subtle stages.

TM markets its mantras as particular sounds or vibrations stemming from a long tradition of knowledge that, according to Maharishi, are known to have life-supporting effects. TM teachers tell students that the mantras do not have any meaning and they are uniquely chosen for each student. But this is not the case.

There are three mantra secrets.

First, the mantras TM sells to people are not actually necessary to meditate. As documented in *Beacon Light of the Himalayas*, Maharishi holding a microphone said that one could use the word "mike" as a mantra. A meditator did not require one of his unique mantras to quiet the mind. Maharishi, by his own words, admitted that they were unnecessary:

> By reducing the sound of the word 'mike' to its subtler and still subtler stages and allowing the mind to go on experiencing all the stages one by one the mind can be trained to be so sharp as to enter into the subtlest stage of the sound mike, transcending which it will automatically get into the realm of Sat-Chidanandam [pure consciousness] and experience it. Thus, we find that any sound can serve our purpose of training the mind to become sharp.[9]

Second, TM mantras, according to Maharishi, invoke the spirits of Hindu gods. While even a word like 'mike' would work, Maharishi proposed that repetition of his mantras offered something unique: they produced special vibrations. Hindu audiences learned that these vibrations attracted the "grace" of a personal Hindu god, "to make us happier in every walk of life." As *Beacon Light of the Himalayas* documents, again in Maharishi's own words:

> But we do not select the sound at random. We do not select any sound like 'mike', flower, table, pen, wail, etc., because such ordinary sounds can do nothing more than merely sharpening the mind; whereas there are some special sounds which have the additional efficacy of producing vibrations whose effects are found to be congenial to our way of life. **This is the scientific reason** why we do not select any word at random. For our practice, **we select only the suitable mantras of personal gods. Such mantras fetch to us the grace of personal gods** and makes us happier in every walk of life. (Bold added.) [10]

TM mantras are meant to create vibrations that arouse and attract those entities to the meditator. For some, this is not an issue, as they might not believe it or simply don't care. Sound vibrations and their effects on consciousness are not unique to TM; they are referenced in many Hindu meditation practices. However, such concepts don't fit neatly within the framework of Western teachings or philosophies, perhaps similar to the meridians in Chinese medicine. Some people, therefore, may dismiss them as nonsense or irrelevant, while others must confront the unpleasant possibility that silent repetition of whatever-it-is may have effects that are not anticipated, understood, or desired.

Tale of Two Meditations: East Is East and West Is West

Maharishi described meditation and the mantra differently when first presenting to an Eastern (Hindu Indian) audience versus a Western (predominately Judeo-Christian) audience. Eastern meditators learn from the start that the mantra is the vehicle to embark on a spiritual journey, which, in Hindu philosophy, is a path to "eternal life—a life of eternal bliss and absolute consciousness." However, when Maharishi came West, Westerners weren't interested in his spiritual message. They wanted relief from stress and Maharishi was more than willing to sell it to them. As recorded in *Beacon Light*, Maharishi spoke openly to his Hindu audience about the spiritual nature of TM. He began his speech on the second day of the gathering by relating that the purpose of chanting mantras and performing other Hindu rituals was to invite the Vedic (Hindu) gods to the conference.[11]

Maharishi told those gathered that they only needed to practice TM twice daily for about fifteen to twenty minutes for three to five years, and the result would be higher consciousness and eternal life. Hindus have always understood that gaining higher consciousness is an arduous path and that few ever achieve it. Maharishi's promise was preposterous, especially given that his own teacher reportedly spent forty years immersed in the most rigorous of acetic practices from the age of nine attempting to achieve it. Maharishi also promised an end to personal suffering, plus the bonus of wealth, within a short time of starting TM. A true guru who followed traditional Hindu practices would never promise material riches, as they are considered a hindrance to spiritual pursuits.

The Last Mantra Secret

The third secret is that a TM student's personally-selected mantra is not all that personal. Mantras are assigned by age (or age and sex, depending on the teacher training course attended). So, if you happen to have a teacher who was trained in 1975, that teacher would have sixteen mantras to choose from. If, instead, your teacher was trained in 1970, chances are you would receive a different mantra, because they would only have eight to choose from (four for men and four for women).

According to early teachers, in 1961, there was only one mantra for everyone. In 1969, Maharishi added eight mantras: four for men and four for women. In 1972, mantras, no longer divided by sex, numbered nine. When I became a teacher in 1975, I received sixteen mantras to assign based on age alone. All children under eleven years old received the same mantra. For those ages twelve to twenty-five, the mantra changed in two-year increments. The interval shifted to five years for people who were twenty-six to fifty-nine. All who were sixty years and older received the same mantra.[12]

A TM teacher posted the following anonymously in the 1990s:

> As TM teachers, we were officially told repeatedly 'the mantras had no meaning for the meditators.'
>
> Like a lot of the language in the TM movement, this was fairly weasel-like. You'll notice that the statement doesn't read, 'the mantras have no meaning.' Most of us as insiders understood this to mean that they had no meaning for the meditators because we didn't tell them the meaning.
>
> We saw tapes of Maharishi where he repeatedly explained that the sounds of the mantras, especially as one approaches transcendence, had the effect of summoning very refined 'impulses of creative intelligence.' In other tapes, he explained that the 'impulses of creative intelligence' or 'laws of nature' were devas such as Indra, Agni, and so forth. He also explicitly said that in the proper state of consciousness, that repeating the name of 'impulses of creative intelligence' in Sanskrit had the effect of creating or summoning the 'form.'

47

Nearly every TM teacher knew from reading 'Beacon Light of the Himalayas,' from other TM teachers, and so forth that the mantras are actually the names or invocations for Hindu devas. In the 70s, *Time* magazine and other publications printed lists of translated mantras. Nearly every teacher had read such articles and knew that the mantras had meaning.

Finally, every TM teacher had to memorize and pass innumerable tests on the word-by-word vocabulary in the puja. So, *every single TM teacher in the world* is well aware that the word 'shri' means 'glorious or self-effulgent,' and 'namah' means 'I bow down.'

So, any TM teacher who tells you that they don't know that the advanced techniques mean 'I bow down to the glorious [deva]' is lying to you. For instance, the technique 'SHRI AING NAMAH' translates as 'I bow down to the glorious AING [Saraswati].'[13]

In 1975, I had a different experience. We were told that the mantras were "sounds without meaning." Maharishi told us that if the mantras had meaning, the mind would stay on the surface and not be able to settle down. While other sounds would work, he chose TM's mantras because, according to his tradition, their effects were known to be life supporting. In videos we viewed, he talked about "impulses of creative intelligence," not about names of Hindu devas or summoning the "form."

I first became aware of the mantra-deity connection a few years after taking the teacher-training course, when I got my first advanced technique. I was told to add the word *namah* to my mantra. By then, I knew that namah meant, "I bow down." (I did not know anything about *Beacon Light of the Himalayas* before conducting research for this book.)

I was disappointed that the mantras were assigned by age and not by some magic aura-reading technique that Maharishi might have taught us. We were instructed to tell students that the mantras were uniquely chosen for them. As teachers, we were supposed to give the impression that we had significantly more mantras than the actual number. Not infrequently, two people sharing the same mantra age category shared their mantra with each other and were always disappointed to discover they had the same one. Some felt lied to or cheated. As teachers, we were always embarrassed when this occurred.

Maharishi, on the other hand, had no compunction about exaggerating the number of mantras. In a 1967 British television interview, broadcast journalist, Sir David Frost, asked him if everyone received the same mantra. Maharishi said, "Oh there are lots of sounds." Frost asked if that meant hundreds or thousands. Maharishi replied, "You could say thousands."[14]

Right to Full Disclosure

"Full disclosure" has become a consumer expectation. Both consumers and consumer law require alerting buyers/users of risks related to a product or service. In addition, there are popular websites, such as Yelp, that allow consumers to report their level of satisfaction with goods and services they have purchased. People have a right to know about a product's dangers and limitations.

In contrast, the way TM is presented to the public is a study in concealment. Poor communicators are not the problem. TM's articulate spokespeople could explain the fine print, so to speak. Robert Roth, executive director of the David Lynch Foundation and a prominent public face of TM in the U.S., is one such example. As a TM teacher for over four decades, he has a solid grasp on what TM is all about.

How, then, does he address the meaning of TM mantras? The following summary is a partial transcription of Roth's lengthy explanation of the mantra from a YouTube video, featured on TM.org:

> [A] mantra has no meaning associated with it, and this is very important because if it had meaning, it would keep the attention on the surface of the mind...If the mantra had any meaning, it would keep us on the surface... I have been asked, 'Aren't mantras the names of Buddhist Deities or Hindu gods or whatever'? And the answer is a flat-out no. There is no meaning associated with the sound. That isn't to say that in any given

language the sound tulip couldn't have a meaning that has been ascribed to it at some later time. But the sound or origin of the mantras in Transcendental Meditation has no meaning associated with it. They are not the names of some deity. They are not the names of anything. They are just a sound.[15]

Someone considering learning TM has the right to information that will allow him or her to make an informed decision. They have the right to know that learning TM requires participating in a Hindu prayer ritual and that TM mantras are the names of Hindu deities. Those responsible for allocating public funds should have the same information. It shouldn't matter if TM is selling spirituality or health; honesty is a fundamental value and expectation of both.

In the West, Maharishi's mantra deceptions continued unabated for forty-nine years—from 1957, when he first left India, until his death in 2008. Today, they are continued by TM teachers around the world.

Chapter 3

What's in a Name?

Those who show you the way can also lead you astray.
Anonymous

Who was Maharishi before he became the guru of TM? When I was with him he was charming, brilliant, and had an extremely sharp wit. Clearly, many people were drawn to him. But, was he ever a spiritual guide in the traditional Hindu sense?

The first clue is a handwritten letter, copied in *Beacon Light of the Himalayas*, dated November 22, 1955, that bears his signature, *Bal Brahmachari Mahesh*. *Bal* or *Bala* refers to the goddess whom the student has taken as his object of devotion. *Brahmachari* indicates the student is celibate, but not a monk.

Only *sanyasis* (ascetics who take vows and wear the orange robes) are legitimately called monks. *Mahesh*, presumably his birth name, is a name of the Hindu god, shiva, meaning "Destroyer [of Ignorance]."[1]

Maharishi's caste limited his religious aspirations, which is perhaps the reason he started out serving as a clerk-secretary for his guru. Soon after the meeting described in *Beacon Light of the Himalayas*, Mahesh began calling himself *Maharishi Bala Brahmachari Mahesh Yogi Maharaj*.

Maharishi, or *Great Seer*, is a title bestowed out of respect on the greatest of India's saints. It would be highly improper for a clerk-secretary, even of a respected guru, to claim such an esteemed designation for himself, but that's exactly what Maharishi did. *Yogi* isn't a title at all, but rather a description of someone who claims to be enlightened. If not bestowed by a worthy Hindu teacher or religious body, calling oneself a yogi is considered boastful.

Maharaj or *Great King* (of the yogis) is a title added to great saints' names. Thus, *Maharishi Bala Brahmachari Mahesh Yogi Maharaj* translates as *The Great Seer, The Enlightened One and Great King*. Maharishi's self-proclaimed titles were likely regarded as blasphemous and ludicrous by anyone familiar with Hinduism.

The documentary *David Wants to Fly* contains an interview conducted by filmmaker David Sieveking with the current Sankaracharya (monastery head) of Jyotirmath, a city in the Northern Indian state of Uttarakhand. The Sankaracharya claims to have been a disciple of Guru Dev, who accepted him in his monastic order. He also claims Maharishi did not belong to the priestly caste and that he was never educated as either a yogi or a spiritual teacher. In the Sankaracharya's opinion, Maharishi had no right to teach meditation because of his caste.

But it was Maharishi's profit motives that elicited the Sankaracharya's most stinging criticism. He said, "A true guru expects nothing from his disciple and never asks anything; instead, the disciple offers service to the guru. Gurus don't sell their knowledge—they share it. In fact," he continued, "Guru Dev had a sign in his ashram that read, 'Donations are not allowed; you can only sacrifice your sins here.'" He concluded the interview by telling Sieveking: "What you have learned from Maharishi will not bring you spiritual progress."[2]

Preacher, Not Practitioner, of Celibacy

Referring to himself as a *Brahmachari* implies that Maharishi was celibate. And while Maharishi encouraged celibacy, he didn't practice it. In 1968, when The Beatles were in India at Maharishi's ashram, John Lennon sensed that the "celibate monk" was behaving inappropriately. He left the ashram, reportedly repulsed by what he perceived as Maharishi's hypocrisy. Subsequently, Lennon and Paul McCartney wrote the song "Sexy Sadie" about Maharishi's alleged indiscretions. They originally named it "Maharishi" but reportedly changed the title at George Harrison's request. As the song goes:

> Sexy Sadie what have you done
> You made a fool of everyone
> You made a fool of everyone
> Sexy Sadie ooh what have you done.
> Sexy Sadie you broke the rules
> Sexy Sadie ooh you broke the rules...
> However big you think you are
> Sexy Sadie ooh you'll get yours yet.[3]

Some months earlier, when Lennon wrote "The Maharishi Song," which was never released on an album, he was less restrained. Some of the lyrics are:

> I knew only one thing:
> He must have had some of his own
> It must have been that little Indian piece
> She came with the tailor
> And could sit at his feet...
> He looked holy
> (But he was a sex maniac)
> I couldn't say that, but he certainly wasn't...
> (Holy)
> In the true sense of the word, that is.[4]

Judith Bourque wrote a book that provides the most detailed account of Maharishi's extracurricular activities. Bourque was twenty-two years old and had traveled to India to become a TM teacher. *Robes of Silk, Feet of Clay* recounts her two-year affair with Maharishi that began in India in 1970, and continued while traveling with him in Europe and the U.S.

After several weeks of sneaking off to be with him, Bourque asked the guru what would happen if she got pregnant. Maharishi's reply was her wake-up call. She writes, "His answer was quick and ruthless,

'Get married... quick.' 'To whom?' I asked. 'Some good choice in the movement.'" She understood then that the relationship would never be anything more than their secret affair for Maharishi. As time went on, he called for her less often. Realizing that his interest had moved on to other young women, she left.[5]

Another former lover described her affair with Maharishi that also began in India in 1969, when she was also twenty-two years old. She asked him about his being a celibate monk, and he reportedly replied, "There are exceptions to every rule." The woman further said, "He was a brilliant manipulator. I just couldn't see that he was a dirty old man. We made love regularly. And I don't think I was the only girl. At one stage I thought I was pregnant by him."[6]

Two personal assistants to Maharishi also recounted the guru's dalliances. One, interviewed in the documentary *David Wants to Fly*, recalled taking women to Maharishi's room. The second, as mentioned in Judith Bourque's book, was close to Maharishi from 1972 to 1976. He told Bourque that he had given the key to Maharishi's room to different women once or twice a week, believing at the time they were handling the mail or doing artwork, or accepting some other vague explanation he was given.

Chapter 4

Religious Roots and Money Motives

What Do You Do When the Well Runs Dry? Teach People How To Fly

After the last wave of interest sparked by Maharishi's appearances on the *Merv Griffin Show* peaked in 1975, fewer people were walking into TM centers. Maharishi quickly understood that he was not going to make a lot of money just from teaching basic meditation. TM instruction wasn't that expensive at the time, and overhead costs including rent, utilities, advertising, and TM teacher salaries, although minimal, added up.

Maharishi responded with a whole new program of advanced meditation techniques, which he called the TM-Sidha program. (Maharishi spelled his trademarked TM-Sidhi and TM-Sidha programs with a single *d*, but the traditional Hindu spellings in English are *siddhi* and *siddha*. The traditional English is used in this book.) Whether consciously or unconsciously, he employed what is today a well-known marketing strategy: focus most of your attention on the people who are already your best customers, and the more loyal the better. Whether aware of this marketing strategy or not, this is exactly what he did. The siddhis were a way to extract money out of his followers. Now he told them they would be able to levitate, become invisible, be enlightened and omniscient, have super vision and hearing, and possess the strength of an elephant, as well as eternal life. Who could possibly resist? (Later, he would sell them vitamins, elixirs, Hindu prayers, gemstones, astrology, and anything else that could be packaged and sold for a profit.)

Speed Enlightenment and Supernatural Powers

Take a minute and close your eyes. Imagine a small gymnasium with a large open floor, covered in several inches of foam padding. There are ten to twelve men dressed in white shirts and white pants, sitting with their legs crossed, bouncing at different intervals across the room. All of them look like they are in the late teens to early twenties, and they're all pretty thin. Some are bouncing a bit higher than others, and some are bouncing a bit faster across the floor. But all of them are expending large amounts of effort to do something that looks ridiculous. Most sane observers might wonder, "What on earth are they up to?" It turns out, according to Maharishi, they were making the world a better place. They are "yogic flyers," and once all the atmospheric stress is reduced (by enough people meditating), they will be able to fly through the air like birds.

Maharishi promised that the siddha (the individual) would be able to control nature, and if enough people (the square root of one percent of the population) practiced the siddhis together, the coherence of their group meditations would dramatically speed up their personal enlightenment, as well as end crime, make nations invincible, and usher in world peace.

In 1977, TM teachers held press conferences in numerous cities throughout the U.S., describing the wonders of the siddhis. Not only did they claim the ability to levitate, they said becoming invisible was also a snap:

'We levitate every day, sometimes twice a day,' TM executive Michael Moore said. 'We can make ourselves invisible too.' But when asked to give a demonstration, Moore and his fellow TM executive governors were a bit shy. 'It looks too much like a circus promotion,' TMer James Weldon said. 'I wouldn't even think of flying around during classes.' Levitation is a very private 'thing,' according to TMer Rod Richards.[1]

56

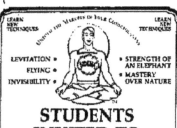

One TM governor explained levitation as being quite simple, saying, "It's just a matter of mind-body coordination. We tell the body to walk, and it walks. Why not tell it to fly?" In response, Steve Mitchell, writing for the *Palm Beach Post*, said, "I suspected it had something to do with (1) gravity and (2) the absence of wings."[2]

When similar stories appeared in newspapers around the country, of course, most people were skeptical. Now, after four decades, not one person has ever demonstrated levitation or any other superpowers Maharishi professed. In hindsight, it is clear those TM representatives were lying through their teeth. But back then, in our eyes, they were special. They had the sidhi techniques, and we wanted them. We never considered that they were lying or using euphemisms for levitation. When TM released photographs of people hanging in mid-air to the media, we believed what we saw. We learned later that the photos were fakes.

When Money and the Truth Collide

In 1981, the Dalai Lama invited Dr. Herbert Benson and a team of scientists to India to document extreme changes in physiology that had been reported during the meditation of Tibetan monks and to measure them using sensitive scientific equipment. With the Dalai Lama's approval, the research team was also permitted to witness an advanced meditative practice, lung gom-pa—literally translated as the ability "to go up and down."

Two monks agreed to demonstrate *lung gom-pa*, but the elder one, who was seventy years old, begged off on the actual levitation. The practice had become too strenuous for him. Thus, as Benson wrote in his book, "The young monk bent his knees slightly, and jumped three to four feet into the air, with his legs straight. While in the air, he rapidly assumed the crossed-legged position and fell to the ground while maintaining this position." Benson affirmed that they witnessed a remarkable athletic performance and commented that if it were spiritual, one would suspect the older monk would have been more proficient. The monks did not know of any person who could levitate in the sense of hovering. Dr. Benson asked the older monk if he would like to have the ability to levitate in that manner. With a twinkle in his eyes, the monk said, "There is no need. We now have airplanes."[3]

If the Dalai Lama's handpicked monks couldn't levitate, what could Maharishi expect from his siddhas? TM teachers were almost all middle-class, Western college students or recent graduates, most of who had only been practicing TM for less than five years.

Maharishi knew from the start that levitation was a total fantasy. Moreover, as smart as the guru was, he must have realized that the entire TM movement would be ridiculed over the wild claims he was making. Why take such a risk? The only logical answer is money. Lots of it.

Maharishi charged a minimum of $3,000 and as much as $10,000 ($40,741 in 2017 dollars) to teach the sidhis. As of June 1977, the *Palm Beach Post* estimated that about 1,500 TMers had taken the course. Since the courses were held at Maharishi International University or in hotels (often cheaply rented during the off-season), with most of the cooking and cleaning done by TM students working for credits to take expensive TM courses, those 1,500 course participants likely netted Maharishi over $25 million in current dollar value (2017). Over the years, thousands more would learn. With that kind of revenue, Maharishi must have considered ridicule of his levitation claims a very minor cost of doing business.

So, what did the package include? When I became a siddha, not much. At the course I attended, I was taught nineteen English words or phrases—TM refers to them as *sutras* (Sanskrit for *string* or *thread*)—to be repeated in sequence. The precise instructions have possibly changed over the years, but the names of the sutras that I learned, all of which were in English, have likely remained the same or are similar to the ones listed here:

Friendliness
Compassion
Happiness
Strength of an elephant
Bronchial tube
Inner light

Sun
Moon
Polestar
Trachea
Navel
Distinction between intellect and transcendence
Transcendence intuition
Transcendence finest hearing
Transcendence finest sight
Transcendence finest taste
Transcendence finest touch
Transcendence finest smell
Relationship of body and akasha-the lightness of cotton fiber

To prepare for the levitation technique (later called *yogic flying* when it became clear that no one would ever actually levitate), the siddha would begin with a twenty-minute TM session and then repeat, "Relationship of body and akasha—lightness of cotton fiber." That phrase would be said two or four times (mentally) with fifteen-second pauses between each repetition. The process continued for five to thirty minutes.

After completing the sutra repetition, the siddha rested for up to thirty minutes and then read a Hindu Scripture (the ninth mandala of the rig veda) for another ten minutes. A glance at a few lines from the text should put to rest any possible doubt as to how Hinduism permeates TM: "Come with food to the sacrifice of the mighty gods, and bring us strength and sustenance. To thee we come, O dropping Soma; for thee only is this our worship day by day, our prayers are to thee, none other."[4]

Before practicing the siddhis, I had a relatively normal life as a TM teacher. We meditated about thirty minutes, twice a day, instead of the standard twenty minutes. We had regular dinners with our kids and often with other TM teachers, many of whom had normal jobs and taught TM part-time. Many of us had kids, so we planned and attended birthday parties and other usual childhood activities. Our children attended regular schools. We watched television and went to movies. I even had a weekly poker game at my house. Every player was a TM teacher and most worked with me at the National TM Center.

As siddhas, the time we committed to meditating jumped from sixty minutes to four hours daily. We had less time for everything, including our kids. For the added effort, I gained nothing. Preparing for the day they would ultimately fly, some people were hopping around, but I wasn't among them. Still, I really wanted the siddhis to work. I wanted to witness someone becoming invisible. But, no one ever did.

Some people talked about bliss when they did the program. The only bliss I experienced was since we worked for the National Center, the course fees (which would have been a fortune for us) were waived. These courses were Maharishi's focus, and many teachers went into debt borrowing several thousands of dollars to attend. Becoming a siddha was the goal of almost every TM teacher.

Even without immediate results, we were willing to give the siddhis time to kick in and assumed that it might take a few years. At the time, TM teachers thought that Maharishi could levitate at will. When asked by journalists or other outsiders why he didn't prove it, a typical response was: "Maharishi is too humble for such a demonstration" or some other deflection.

James Randi authored *Flim Flam*, a book that exposes occult and false scientific claims. He also co-founded The Committee for Skeptical Inquiry and founded the James Randi Educational Foundation. Through the foundation, Randi extended an offer: a million dollars to any TM practitioner (or anyone) who could levitate. No one claimed the prize.[5]

Unless he began to believe his fairy tales, Maharishi knew that his promises about levitation would never take off. Instead of admitting the truth, he blamed the high level of stress in the world for the failure to launch.

The Giggling Guru and His Flying Yogis

If the siddhas weren't levitating, then what were they doing during their morning and evening program? Like bouncing torsos, they were (and have been ever since) crossing their legs and hopping around on foam pads. I remember conversations with fellow siddhas about the different density levels of the foam pads. It was all about density; the denser the foam, the higher the bounce.

What compelled people to continue butt hopping when no one was levitating? As previously mentioned, Maharishi simply said that butt hopping, a.k.a. yogic flying, was the first stage of levitation. No wonder Maharishi was often referred to as the "Giggling Guru"—he was giggling at what a bunch of absolute fools he'd created, including me. People not only treated him like a god incarnate, but also tortured their bodies while making him wealthy and adored beyond his wildest dreams.

What Enlightenment Will Cost You Today

After two months, a meditator is eligible to receive an advanced technique. The stated purpose of the technique is to deepen the meditation experience and speed up enlightenment. I remember adding the word *shri* to the beginning of another mantra, one that I was familiar with, but wasn't the one I had been using. Also, the Sanskrit word *namah* was added at the end.

Getting an advanced technique requires another initiation, another puja, and, of course, another fee. I remember that seven advanced techniques were available when I taught TM, but I recently learned from a TM governor that, currently, four are in use.

When I taught TM in the 1970s, the minimum interval between advanced techniques was eighteen months. At some point, Maharishi reduced the interval to six months, likely with the intent to speed up cash flow. Recently, the wait time has dropped to two months. Prices for advanced techniques and basic TM instruction are about the same, currently $960.

Siddha Course

Today, one can become a siddha for approximately $5,000 (according to the Beverly Hills TM Center) plus travel and housing expenses. The course requires three preparatory weekends in classes at a local

TM center and two weeks in residence at the Maharishi University of Management in Fairfield, Iowa, or some other location. Participants likely learn the same sutras that, for over forty years, have failed to facilitate levitation or any of the other superhuman powers. Siddhas meditate four hours a day.

Governors

The next level of advancement—becoming a governor—currently costs $19,500 (according to the Beverly Hills TM Center) plus travel expenses for a five-month-long, in-residence training course. Upon passing the class, governors earn the privilege of working full-time for the organization as TM teachers. They receive minimal pay and enjoy few, if any, employment benefits.

In 2005, Maharishi decided that anyone who wanted to teach TM or work full-time for the organization must be recertified every five years. I do not know the cost of the recertification course; however, regular tune-ups are required to maintain it. Tune-ups are billed in fifteen-minute increments. In 2006, the fifteen-minute sessions were $50 each. A recertified governor's TM program increases to six hours a day.

Rajas

The next level up is the raja program. For its price alone—one million U.S. dollars—this package is likely the most expensive course in history. When Maharishi was alive, buyers gained access to him for three weeks via closed-circuit television while he was upstairs in his quarters in the same building. Why they didn't encounter their guru in-person is only known to his inner circle of attendants. Was Maharishi too frail at that point to risk direct contact, which could raise questions about his physical health, or, one must wonder, his sanity?

Rajas enjoy special perks. Besides extra-advanced techniques, they have the privilege of wearing a special costume; including a gold crown, white robes, and necklaces. They also get a title. They are referred to as *rajas* (or *one who rules*) and are addressed as *His Excellency, His Highness* or *His Majesty* by other TMers. Each one has bought the right to run a small country—or a few states in a larger country—within the TM fantasy world, known as the Global Country of World Peace (GCWP).

Maharishi personally crowned the current head of the GCWP, Tony Nader, a Lebanese-born physician, and designated him as his successor. Now known as His Majesty Maharaja Adhiraj Raja Raam, Nader resides at TM's headquarters in a 200-room palace in Vlodrop, Holland. The building conforms to Maharishi's interpretation of Vedic (ancient Hindu) architecture.

Peace Palaces and Cosmic Government

On April 22, 2009, WikiLeaks released the "Transcendental Meditation Governor Recertification Course Overview and Policies" that TM internally described as an "unofficial" document that summarized the policies and procedures outlined in the official 2005 Governor Recertification Course. The stated goal was to hasten the development of Peace Palaces, TM centers that would teach TM and also include massage parlors and spas. They would also sell Maharishi-branded products, such as medicinal supplements, elixirs, vitamins, and herbal remedies.

Leaders of TM

His Majesty Maharaja Adhiraj Raja Raam, aka Dr. Tony Nader, First
Sovereign Ruler of the Global Country of World Peace designated
by Maharishi in 2008 as his successor

The introduction to the document includes a quote from Maharishi's opening address to participants in which he described his vision of a utopian land of make-believe, complete with a Constitution of the Universe and Cosmic Government on Earth. His words illustrate how self-absorbed he had become in the few years before his death.

Maharishi said that his rajas were the representatives of Divine Intelligence; the shining stars that played a parental role for their people, setting all life in the evolutionary direction. They would rule "Heaven on Earth," as he expressed, "This will be the Peace Government, as the government of Nature administers a very concrete galactic universe, but very peacefully. We are going to be a practical channel of the Cosmic Government on Earth. We are going to be the administrators of Heaven on Earth."[6]

The pledge, signed by his recertified governors, further reveals the extent to which he openly embraced Hinduism as well as the fantasy world he had succumbed to towards the end of his life:

> I will take all these steps so that, on this *Guru Purnima*, the full moon of July 2005, my city will welcome the descent of Heaven on Earth—the descent of *Satya Yuga* saying bye-bye to *Kali Yuga*.
>
> I pay homage to Guru Dev and the Holy tradition of Vedic Masters through all the levels of Rajas and Maharaja of the Global Country of World Peace—the State Rajas, the National Rajas and the Global Maharaja—reaching the holy tradition of Vedic Masters whose guiding light, His Divinity Brahmananda Sarasvati, has blessed the world with this whole knowledge of Enlightenment to the individual and Invincibility to the nation.[7]

What Has TM Become?

The Australian version of *60 Minutes* ran a segment on TM that is currently viewable on YouTube and allows you to judge for yourself. The interview set-up was similar to the million-dollar raja course. Maharishi answered questions via closed-circuit TV from a room only one floor up from the *60 Minutes* crew, and based upon how the exchange unfolded, someone in the TM organization made a wise decision to create a barrier.[8]

No longer appearing as the gentle, likable, sharp-witted leader, Maharishi appeared as a mean-spirited megalomaniac, surrounded by fools and buffoons. He was neither gracious nor humble. He sounded irritated and inconvenienced throughout the interview. He mockingly denied that The Beatles had anything to do with putting TM on the world map.

A main topic of the show, yogic flying, made the guru and his handlers fly off the handle. After one of the TM organization's top leaders explained yogic flying, the *60 Minutes* interviewer termed the explanation "gobbledygook." When he later asked Maharishi if he could fly, Maharishi was so outraged at the perceived impertinence of the question that he halted the interview and demanded that the reporter and film crew be thrown out immediately. From the start, Maharishi conveyed that merely talking with him was a privilege and taking precious time from his work of building a perfect man and making nations invincible.

Slicing and Dicing Hinduism

Second only to *Beacon Light of the Himalayas*, the Governor Recertification Course guidelines open a wide window to the Hindu soul of TM. They also include Maharishi's marching orders to his elite troops. The essence of his message was sell every part of the Hindu religion that could be a profit center.

TM: The Supreme Authority on Health

In the recertification guidelines, Maharishi delivers a stern warning to his cosmic administrators regarding medical practitioners: "We are not going to take help from medical Drs. as medical professionals give poison. So don't engage any medical Drs. for anything—absolutely whatever it is—even if they are in our Movement family." As he noted in his proclamation to TM governors, "Hold onto the fact that we are the supreme authorities on health—we know how to create perfect health…"[9]

Of course, Maharishi made a distinction between actual medical intervention for an illness—something he was against—and grabbing endorsements from medical practitioners, especially from famous ones like Dr. Mehmet Oz. Doctors in the "Movement family" were only useful to promote Maharishi's agenda.[10]

Organic Melodies for your Vedic Bliss Veggies

Agriculture inspectors might be interested to learn that the term "organic" in the TM world includes growing produce with piped-in Vedic melodies that make fruit and vegetables more nutritious and supports "bliss, enlightenment, and invincibility." Naturally, bliss-infused veggies are much more expensive. Possibly anticipating some blowback on pricing, Maharishi advised, "Advertise as Vedic Organic, and explain that this higher price covers the cost of growing the produce with Vedic melodies."[11]

A Harmonious Universe: Individual Physiology, Cosmic Consciousness and The Galactic Body

Living completely and harmoniously within the TM universe also requires living in Vastu, or Maharishi Sthapatya Veda. Some might label *Vastu* as feng shui on steroids, requiring the proper orientation of a building, correct placement of rooms in the correct proportions, as well as incorporating many other elements. No one could accuse Maharishi of thinking small. Maharishi defined *sthapatya* at the Governor Recertification Course:

> The individual consciousness administers the individual body. The Cosmic consciousness administers the physiology of the galactic body. If the relationship between individual and cosmic consciousness is not harmonious, then there is discomfort, or disease, in the individual physiology.
>
> It is therefore necessary to establish an unbreakable relationship between…the individual body and the cosmic body through Sthapatya-Veda.[12]

Maharishi envisioned the largest demolition/reconstruction program in world history, and his cosmic administrators would be in charge. He told them they were going to rebuild the world in every way and this huge undertaking would require them to inspire all builders to reconstruct all cities, even building new cities beside existing cities. He also told them that remodeling was basically a waste of time because it was hard to get the angles just right. However, this was actually a good thing because the billions flowing through demolition projects should flow through the intelligence of his recertified governors.[13]

Closer to home, next to its world headquarters in Vlodrop, Holland, the TM organization has been fighting the Dutch authorities for permission to tear down an adjacent monastery, a centuries-old historic landmark, because it does not face the "right" direction. The monastery's entrance is twenty-nine degrees off.[14]

Yagyas: Pay to Pray

A *yagya* is a Hindu devotion achieved through chanting Vedic mantras. The TM organization encourages the purchase of yagyas to influence and enliven Hindu gods (*devatas*). In the TM world, Maharishi established specially trained *pundits*—sometimes referred to as *pandits*—to perform the chants to create peace and prosperity for the individual(s) who sponsor(s) them and for the entire world.

It seems these particular gods are very fond of money. The guru encouraged people to spend as much money as possible on a yagya to get the greatest response from the gods. The donation level was tied to the intensity of the problem and the speed of achieving objectives. He said, "vitta sakhyam na kaaryet," which roughly translates as "do not perform yagyas below one's financial capacity."[15]

In addition to promoting yagyas for the well-being of a country, a TM yagya website offers chants for birthdays, wedding days, wedding anniversaries, the birth of a child, and more. Two donation levels within each category range from $1,000 to $3,000 (recently reduced from $10,000).[16]

For a price comparison, I contacted the Malibu Hindu Temple and asked the cost of a yagya for someone with health and financial problems. The representative replied that the yagya could be performed for a $151 donation to the Temple. In response to my question about long-distance yagyas, she explained that when a yagya was performed on behalf of an individual, the person was required to be present for the ceremony.

The Brahmasthan of India

Maharishi established the Brahmasthan of India as the center of TM's pundit program and referred to it as the holiest place in India. TM followers have reportedly contributed over $100 million to build the facility and provide for the pundits. The complex is in a remote area of India. One hundred million dollars goes a lot further in India than in the U.S., so it would seem that the money raised should have been more than adequate to build and maintain the complex as well as the pundit program. It wasn't.

Filmmaker David Sieveking attempted to tour the Brahmasthan for his documentary about TM, *David Wants to Fly*. When a guard prevented his entrance, he changed into robes, applied body paint, and posed as a Western holy man. Not only did he get in, he convinced the guard to give him a tour. To maintain his disguise, Sieveking couldn't bring his production crew inside to film. As a result, only the exterior of the mostly deserted Brahmasthan was filmed. Those views showcase an eerie ghost town. Sieveking said it reminded him of a vacant Hollywood set. While there, he counted only eight pundits and reported that the guard told him only a few pundits lived at the facility.[17]

Sieveking was also allowed to film the first raja meeting at TM's Vlodrop headquarters following Maharishi's death. Aside from capturing on film a major power struggle at the meeting challenging the leadership of Maharishi's anointed successor, there was a report on the Brahmasthan. One raja reported that the organization was in the midst of a $400 million fundraising campaign to permanently house 8,000 pundits. There was still work to do, as only $200 million had been raised to date. He also told those assembled that he and his wife planned to move there once construction was completed and the 8,000 pundits moved in.[18]

Trouble in Maharishi Vedic City

While the Brahmasthan in India may be desolate, bigger problems have been brewing at TM's pundit operation in Vedic City, U.S.A.— i.e., Fairfield, Iowa. For several years, the Vedic City pundits remained out of sight; few people were aware of their existence in barrack-style housing, which was down an unmarked road and behind a fenced enclosure. A guard was posted at the entrance of the barracks to keep the pundits in, and the curious out.

In January 2014, the *India Today* newspaper reported a "shocking revelation." Of 1,050 young Indians who had been brought to Maharishi Vedic City, at least 163 had gone missing in the prior year. The paper reported that the pundits had been recruited through literature distributed in poor Indian villages, where they were promised a high school education, after which they would be trained as "masters of Hindu religious rites and services."

According to the report, the education provided was rarely above the fifth-grade level, but that was the least of the issues. Young Indian men were transported to Iowa on visas that allowed them to remain in the U.S. for two years with a possible six-month extension. TM authorities required that they surrender their passports when they arrived. The pundits were not allowed to leave the barracks. They earned $50 per month, with an additional $150 per month paid either to them or their parents in India at the end of two years. Payment reportedly required a pundit's good behavior during the contract term. The article further stated that the contract was drafted in English and not translated or explained to the recruits or their families.[19]

Besides the meager pay, isolation, and living conditions, what could possibly cause the pundits to go missing? According to William Goldstein, Dean of Global Development and General Counsel to the Maharishi University of Management, they appear to have been induced to leave by individuals providing false information of high paying jobs, or by unscrupulous employers taking advantage of them.[20]

Meanwhile, despite all who disappeared with their passports left behind, the Indian consulate in Chicago reported that the Global Country of World Peace (GCWP) (the arm of TM that was responsible for the young men) never sent the missing pundits' passports to the consulate as required by the State Department, nor did it provide any missing persons information to the appropriate authorities. And according to the sheriff's and police departments of Fairfield, Iowa, no missing persons reports were ever filed with them either.[21]

On March 11, 2014, about eighty pundits at Vedic City rioted by shaking, vandalizing, and throwing rocks at a sheriff's truck. A news team from a local television station captured the aftermath of the uprising. Reportedly, the pundits were upset that the sheriff was removing one of their friends to be sent back to India. The sheriff said arrests would have been made had his video camera been working. Without a video, he stated he could not positively identify Maharishi's professional peacemakers who had threatened him and damaged his car.[22]

Five months later, Ajit Panday, having fled the GCWP pundit program, was brutally murdered outside an Atlanta food store where he had been working fifteen-hour shifts. Ajit was reportedly the sole breadwinner in his family. According to the article, no one at GCWP took responsibility to send Ajit's remains back to his distraught, widowed mother in India. Among those not helping was Maharishi's nephew in India, who heads global operations of the sponsoring university.[23]

Where Have All the Pundits Gone?

After the pundit riot, Fairfield's mayor, Ed Malloy, called for more transparency about how the program operated. Perhaps as a result of the negative publicity and outside attention to the program, almost all the pundits were sent back to India. According to one recent report, fewer than twenty-five pundits are still living in Vedic City, down from 1,000 before the riot.[24]

Maharishi Jyotish Program

Maharishi Jyotish, Maharishi's private-label astrology technology, is another program not found on the mainstream TM.org website. Maharishi described *jyotish* as "a precious discipline of my Vedic Science." He also called it a science of technology and consciousness that, in his view, "commands authority over the whole range of the ever-expanding universe." It explains how planets and stars determine how and when positive or negative influences come back to a person as a result of past actions. In other words, Maharishi took the Indian concept of "karma," dressed it up by calling it a science, and turned it into another profit center. Maharishi claimed that his jyotish experts could scientifically predict the future by just knowing one point in the sequence of time. And of course, according to Maharishi, among its attributes, jyotish contributes enlightenment and invincibility to individuals and any nation (willing to pay the fees). Current services and prices are listed below:

- Birth chart or horoscope, a prerequisite for most jyotish services – $400
- Additions to the birth chart – $300, per relative
- Jyotish consultations (one-to-three-year predictions and ability to ask three to ten questions, made by experts based on the birth chart), recommended regularly – $150, per every fifteen minutes
- Muhurta (auspicious starting times for any new activity) – $150 to $300 each
- Compatibility analysis for people considering marriage or business partnerships – $300 for a fifteen-minute consultation
- Auspicious name (the first syllable for a baby's name) – $200
- Ascertaining correct birth time within a span of four hours if no birth certificate is available – $600
- Yagya recommendations (included in all the above services) if purchased individually – $150 (This fee is only to recommend which yagyas to purchase, not the prayer service itself.) [25]

Going Professional: TM Nuns and Monks

The Mother Divine (the nuns of TM) and the Purusha (the monks of TM), devote their lives to carrying out Maharishi's cosmic plan.

Those fully immersed live TM twenty-four hours a day. They have exceptionally long meditation schedules, perform different movement tasks, and reportedly practice celibacy (even among married couples). As a matter of fact, Maharishi strongly encouraged married couples to refrain from intimacy. Celibacy, he said, was the highest form of married life. Possibly having one's hormones and energy depleted by endless meditation, a strict vegetarian diet, and Maharishi-branded medicinal products and elixirs make separation more acceptable.

Mother Divine: The Celibate Nuns of TM

Well beyond meditating at home, girls and women, both single and married, who delve into TM learn that they may embark upon a "blissful life in freedom, fullness, and enlightenment" through various aspects of the Mother Divine Program. According to the website that the TM organization employs to promote such engagements, various weekend and longer-term immersions (described as "retreats," "heaven on earth assemblies," "a taste of blissful life," and so forth) are available for $225 per night, and $1,250 per month in the U.S., Thailand, and Switzerland.[26]

A getaway with the gals to meditate and dine on vegetarian cuisine might seem harmless and pleasant, but depending on the individual and her level of continuing involvement, problems might arise for participants in Mother Divine. One woman was concerned about an in-law enrolled in the Thousand-Headed Mother Divine (THMD) program, a minimum three-month, in-residence commitment for female TM governors. She described her observations of the relative and her friends when they were visiting on a brief leave from a TM campus in Livingston Manor, New York: "Our guests are strange beyond belief," the individual expressed online. "We really feel like they are already trying to make our children feel like we are unworthy parents, and they along with TM are the only way to save them from a miserable future." Having known the in-law for nearly twenty years, the writer said:

> [she'd] observed the [relative's] rapid decline in her behav-
> ior and ability to deal with the outside world since she moved

to Livingston Manor. Her manners have deteriorated to an unbelievable point so that she even eats with her hands now. Having been raised as a Catholic, I am very familiar with the Carmelite Nuns. I mentioned to my husband that she seemed as detached from the world as they are. She is painfully thin, anorexic I would say…Her attitude towards any negative comment about MMY [Maharishi] or the movement is to instantly remove herself angrily from the room. After my brief attempt to get her to discuss the progression of TM from 'World Peace' to where it is now did not produce a discussion as I had hoped. Tonight, she refused to sleep under my roof and moved into the hotel with the rest of the TM relatives...

"Personally," the writer admitted, "I am grateful that she is not here. She eats Maharishi supplements all day long, her hair is falling out, and she has a vacant look in her eyes."

In addition to meditating eight-plus hours daily, the writer described rigid schedules that demanded rising before dawn and being in bed before ten o'clock at night, that she considered as a means of controlling mind and body. Also, she revealed,

"There are many 'silences' observed during the year, the 'month' being the longest. To our knowledge, the silences are just that—a month-long period during which the nuns do not speak. Maharishi reportedly said that prolonged silence 'warms the soul.' It can also have some of the same effects of solitary confinement in breaking down ego barriers, increasing suggestibility, and the like."[27]

Also, akin to Catholic nuns, who are assigned jobs, Mother Divine members must work for TM. A stark difference, however, is that Catholic nuns don't pay money to dedicate their lives to the church. According to course fees shown on the Mother Divine website as of this writing, a TM nun would pay close to $4,000 for her three months of devotion.[28]

Maharishi Purusha: The Monks of TM

Along with recruiting and grooming women as TM nuns, the organization also engages men at progressively deeper levels with the Maharishi Purusha Program. According to the website PurushaCourses. org, Maharishi launched the program in 1981, targeting single men involved in TM and TM-Sidhi courses "who wish to dedicate themselves fully to the most rapid pace of evolution possible."[29]

Maharishi, in fact, referred to Purusha as a profession. Pushing for "a longer practice of the TM and TM-Sidhi program," the program promises "an all-time enjoyment of bliss, freedom, self-sufficiency, invincibility, and spontaneous radiation of a powerful influence on positivity, harmony, happiness, and peace in the environment." In addition to meditating, participants attend "knowledge meetings" and activities "dedicated to enlivening the Silent Administration of Natural Law throughout the world."[30]

Maharishi Mahesh Yogi's successor Maharaja Adhiraj Rajaraam, center, blesses his followers

Chapter 5

TM's Real Golden Boy

While His Majesty, Maharaja Adhiraj Raja Raam, may wear the gold crown, in my opinion, Bob Roth deserves to be wearing it.

Bob Roth describes himself as a world authority on TM. And, there is no doubt he is. He has been a TM teacher for over forty years, written two books on the subject, and is often called upon to teach celebrities and corporate leaders. He is the co-founder and chief executive officer of the David Lynch Foundation, working closely with David Lynch to promote TM.

He is so valued by the TM organization, that on November 9, 2009, Maharishi University of Management awarded him a Ph.D., "Doctorate of World Peace Honoris Causa." The degree itself enumerates some of his qualities such as his being:

> ...Infectiously enthusiastic, boundlessly energetic, ever joyful and youthful, intensely charming, a best friend to all, a brilliant teacher and speaker - all in the cause of the highest and most noble purposes on earth - par excellence a devotee of Maharishi and Guru Dev and an extremely effective exponent of their Total Knowledge and techniques.[1]

Roth has also been effective in downplaying TM's religious underpinnings. And in doing so, he has been instrumental in convincing some people to learn TM who might have chosen not to learn it had they been given all the relevant information. This recently happened to a friend of mine.

My wife and I were at dinner with a couple we know. I mentioned that I was writing a book on TM, and I immediately realized that I had struck a nerve. It turns out the woman had started TM a few months earlier, and Bob Roth was her teacher. She said learning TM had been one of the more disturbing experiences in her life.

After the introductory lecture, and before instruction, she told Roth that she was a religious Jewish woman and did not want to do anything that conflicted with her religion. She asked him to promise her that there was nothing about TM that would conflict with her firmly held beliefs. She said he assured her there was no conflict; he told her that hundreds of clergy of all religions practiced TM, that there was absolutely nothing religious about it, and that she didn't have to believe in anything to do TM. When he led her into the room set up for instruction, she saw the altar and incense and said she felt confused. Not wanting to make a scene, she sat through the puja and was given a mantra. When she repeated her mantra, it sounded familiar to her. Roth assured her it was a meaningless sound. She said she repeated the mantra a few times, but it didn't feel right, so she switched to a Hebrew word and felt more comfortable.[2]

In the documentary, *David Wants to Fly*, Roth meets with the director, David Sieveking. They are in the lobby of a Manhattan hotel to set the ground rules for a ten-minute interview by Sieveking with David Lynch. Roth tells Sieveking, "David is not interested, to be perfectly blunt in the stories that people make up stuff that TM is a cult or a religion because it's not. There are people, my age largely, in the U.S., one or two people, just being completely straightforward here - oh it's a religion, it's a money-making cult, Maharishi mind control." As Roth continues speaking, he asks for the camera to be turned off.[3]

Roth has been a central player in the TM world for decades. Does he genuinely believe that only one or two people in their late sixties think TM is a religion or a cult?

As quoted in Chapter 2 of this book, Roth denies that TM mantras are anything other than meaningless sounds: "But the sound or origin of the mantras in Transcendental Meditation has no meaning associated with it...They are just a sound."[4] However, there is a problem. Earlier in that same chapter, Maharishi himself contradicts Roth. There, I quote Maharishi admitting that TM mantras are selected because they are suitable mantras of personal gods that fetch the grace of those gods. It seems unlikely that Mr. Roth was unaware that Maharishi believed the vibrations of his chosen mantras attracted the grace of Hindu gods.

Roth has written two books on TM. The first, *TM - Transcendental Meditation*, first published in 1997 and revised in 2011, reads like a marketing brochure for TM. It is an uncritical review of mostly decades-old research that should have been updated in a new edition. Roth says he selected eighty-two studies out of over five hundred existing at the time that had been "published in leading, peer-reviewed scientific journals."[5] The most recent studies listed were from 1994 and were seventeen years old when the book was revised in 2011. Much of the research is even older—the majority of it dating back to the 1970s. The balance of the book consists of testimonials, a general description how TM works, and it provides information on how to find a TM teacher. Several reviewers of the book on Amazon expressed disappointment that instead of learning how to do TM, as they thought the book's title implied, they were referred to TM centers where they would have to pay for TM training.[6]

One chapter of the book consists of questions posed and answered by Roth. One question is, "Will my practice of Transcendental Meditation conflict with my religion?" Roth answers, "No, it will enhance your religion. Millions of people of all religions - including clergy of all religions - practice Transcendental Meditation. They report that the technique, by increasing energy and intelligence and eliminating stress and fatigue, allows them to better follow the tenets of their own religion. Transcendental Meditation is a technique, pure and simple. It involves no religion, belief, philosophy, or change in lifestyle."[7]

What does Roth mean by this? What does energy, intelligence, stress, and fatigue have to do with religion? Does he mean you can pray better if you're not tired? Perhaps. But do people with less stress or more energy become more observant in their religious traditions? On Sunday, do energetic Christians choose to go to church instead of riding a bike or going to a movie? TM's endless repetition that "TM makes X better" doesn't mean it's true, including when X is religion.

And what difference does it make if clergy of various religions learned TM? Most likely they believed TM wasn't a religion because some TM teacher told them that it wasn't. I've known two Rabbis that learned TM. One of them officiated at my wedding, and I'm sure there are many others. However, without being able to offer any proof, I believe that if clergymen were told up front what the mantras were and the purpose of the puja ceremony, few, if any, would have started. And I believe even fewer would have started if they knew they could get the benefits they were seeking from a meditation that was secular instead of one pretending to be so, as well as saving a thousand dollars.

While few of the clergy who learned TM are likely familiar with the puja/mantra issues because they were hidden from them, I would venture that almost all of them are familiar with a verse from Leviticus, "You shall not put a stumbling block before the blind." There are many approaches to understanding this verse. In one commentary, blind refers to someone lacking specific information or a proper understanding of a given situation, and a stumbling block means giving misleading information to that person that will result in a mistake. Sometimes giving someone misleading information is entirely innocent, but the consequences for the one receiving and acting on it can, at times, be very painful. How much worse is it when the misinformation is deliberate?

Now, Roth has written a new book, *Strength in Stillness: The Power of Transcendental Meditation*. The book's promotional information on Amazon states:

> Roth breaks down the science behind meditation in a new, accessible way. He highlights the three distinct types of meditation—focused attention, open monitoring, and self-transcending—and showcases the evidence that the third, Transcendental Meditation, is the most effective and efficient

way to reduce stress, access inner power, and build resilience. Free of gimmicks, mystical verbiage, and over-inflated research studies, *Strength in Stillness* is a simple and straightforward guide to calming mind, body, and spirit.[8]

Roth states that TM is the best meditation because of "self-transcending." There are several problems with this, the first being that in everyday language, "transcendence" means "going beyond," and "self-transcendence" means going beyond a prior form or state of oneself. Mystical experience is thought of as a particularly advanced state of self-transcendence, in which the sense of a separate self is abandoned.[9] So is TM secular or is it religious? Perhaps this accounts for why Amazon categorizes Roth's book under the "religion-spirituality" section.

Transcending in Maharishi's world view, at least before he realized how much money could be made selling health, was a spiritual practice that he promised would lead to enlightenment. Initially, he claimed the timeframe for enlightenment was three to five years. When that didn't work, he increased it to five to seven years. The enlightenment time frame is now sixty years and counting. Perhaps TM has a lot of enlightened people in the fold. If so, it is hiding them very well.

Another problem for Roth's thesis that self-transcending makes TM better than other meditations is that Maharishi said that his mantras weren't needed to transcend. As quoted in Chapter 2, Maharishi states that the sound value of any word, appropriately used—by which he meant an effortless, non-focused manner, (basically the entire TM technique in a nutshell)—will allow the mind to experience that sound in subtler and subtler states of awareness, until it transcends.[10] If that's the case, why would anyone need TM for self-transcendence?

As to Roth's claim that the book is free of "mystical verbiage," and "over-inflated research," TM saves the mystical for advanced courses. And, if true, Roth could be the most senior person in the TM organization to admit that TM research is overinflated.

There is no question that TM uses celebrity exceptionally well. The release date for Roth's book is February 6, 2018, and the release party will be a star-studded event in New York, hosted by Hugh Jackman and Tom Hanks. Other celebrities and business leaders have already highly praised the book, with some also expressing their love and admiration for Roth himself. They include Ray Dalio, Arianna Huffington, Oprah Winfrey, Cameron Diaz, Lena Dunham, Michael Fox, and Ellen DeGeneres.

TM uses two of three methods described in a recent article examining how biases develop and help spread misinformation.[11] One is a personal referral. People tend to value the information offered by good friends over all other sources. Advertisers have long recognized that celebrity endorsements are the next best thing to hearing about something from a good friend. This is the reason celebrity endorsements are critical to TM.

The second method is "constant repetition." Constant repetition in the TM world can seemingly have a kind of hypnotic effect. Convincing people TM isn't religion just by saying so over and over has worked very well. So has convincing thousands of people that jumping up and down like some strange frog is "flying." But through constant repetition, this ridiculous activity becomes "yogic flying—the first stage of levitation." That first stage has lasted over forty-two years with no end in sight.

Roth has another big hurdle in making his case for the preeminence of self-transcendence. Judging from the number of meditation studies underway, there is far more interest in both mindfulness and the Relaxation Response than in TM. But the real hurdle for TM is its inability to compete with the burgeoning mindfulness movement. Consider there are hundreds, perhaps now closing in on a thousand, mindfulness-related smartphone apps. Headspace is the biggest one; it is approaching twenty million downloads. There are many other apps with millions of downloads. Most are based on short, guided meditations, stress reduction exercises, and focused attention. Most are simple, secular, require no special initiation, and cost very little in comparison to TM. Some have an inexpensive monthly fee. Many of them are free.

How many TM apps are there? I didn't find any. Perhaps the reason is that TM costs almost a thousand dollars, requires a puja to learn, not to mention pre and post TM instruction meetings that are also required. The main meditation game is online apps and video introductions to mindfulness, and TM is not in that game.

On June 17, 2017, the *Wall Street Journal* ran a feature story on Mr. Roth. I was surprised at how unquestioning the journalist was, as I would have expected a more rigorous analysis of Roth's statements about TM from the *Journal*. At the time, I was midway through researching this book, and for the second or third time in my life, I commented on an article. My comment brought many responses both defending and opposing TM. One responder was Mr. Roth himself. That led to an exchange between us that I believe illustrates the obfuscation that, to me, appears to be TM's default position. The point of this exercise is to showcase that Mr. Roth had numerous opportunities to refute any of the points I made about TM being religious. He didn't.

My first comment:

I was a TM teacher who worked for the National TM office for 5 years in the 1970s. It is disappointing that the *Journal* would publish an article without due diligence. While promoting a safe meditation practice to alleviate stress, TM conceals that Maharishi chose mantras that he said were the names of Hindu gods. The initiation ceremony—the event during which a person first receives his or her mantra—takes place in a candlelit, incense-filled room with a TM teacher chanting Sanskrit prayers before an altar. At the conclusion, the inductee bows before the altar. The altar holds offerings that the student brought to the ceremony and the teacher used to worship Maharishi's predeceased teacher. Every monotheistic religion considers this idol worship. All this was documented by the New Jersey courts which tossed TM from the public schools in that state.

People can do what they choose. They should have honest information, which TM withholds from them.[12]

Mr. Roth's response:

TM is not a religion. Over 8 million people of all religions practice TM. It is taught in public schools, on military bases, and in large and small businesses. In each case, a team of legal experts has done due diligence and researched the accusations and claims and found them to have no basis. The National Institutes of Health has provided over $26 million in grants to study the benefits of TM on heart disease and high blood pressure and the American Heart Association recently stated that TM alone among all meditation practices could be considered effective in reducing hypertension. The $1000 course fee (for adults--for kids it is $360) covers a lifetime of personal instruction and follow up. You pay more than that for a 6-month membership at a yoga studio. Plus, there are scholarships, grants and loans for those who cannot afford the tuition. And the Foundation has provided more than 500,000 people with scholarships so they can learn for free.

There are several problems with Roth's response and those responses that follow. He responds to direct questions with vague statements and deflections. Roth begins with the statement, "TM is not a religion," and he simply repeats that statement throughout our dialogue. He never gives any evidence for his declaration. It's similar in some ways to how fake news that is constantly repeated too often becomes widely believed. My take on what Roth is saying is, "When I tell you TM isn't a religion, you should believe me because I'm a nice person. I'm enthusiastic and assertively keen, and we are all really nice people. We only want to do good, and our goals for the world are truly wonderful. So please ignore the puja. Just TRUST ME, chanting in ancient Sanskrit before a portrait of a glowing guru, burning incense, and making Hindu offerings is NOT a religion. TM is NOT a religion."

As discussed earlier, incessant repetition of catchwords is not something TM invented. It just uses them well. It also uses repetition as a primary advertising tactic. At least for me, a one-time visit to TM's main website resulted in pop-up advertising on almost every page I visited. Sometimes two or three pop-ups appear on the same page. Distractions from the main issue—sidestepping counter arguments rather than refuting them—are staples of propaganda, at least the kind that is intended to spread misinformation.

Roth writes that over eight million people currently practice TM. I have no idea how many people over the past fifty years learned TM, but eight million seems like a major exaggeration. There is no way for an outsider to get a real number because, for many organizations dedicated to self-promotion, bigger is almost always better. Certainly millions of people have learned TM over the last sixty years, but the number of people who stopped could be as high as 90-95 percent. If TM wanted to know what the approximate percentage was, they could find out. That they haven't done so may indicate they are not confident in a good result. Personally, I've known dozens of people who started TM through the years; to the best of my knowledge, no one is currently regular in their practice.

Roth simply ignores my comment on the mantra and TM's Hindu-based initiation ceremony, as if the number of people of different religions who started TM has any bearing whatsoever on whether TM is a religious practice or not. Without presenting any evidence, he asserts that legal teams have researched accusations against TM as a religion and found them baseless. In his various responses, Roth raises many issues attempting to deflect rather than respond to the question of religion. These include claims about TM benefits. I responded to each claim in detail in the *Journal* comments. However, since TM's flawed, biased, and exaggerated research claims are detailed in Chapter 6, with one exception, I didn't include my responses to his various assertions here. The exception is Roth's mischaracterization of the American Heart Association (AHA) study. The AHA said that, due to the lack of data, they couldn't recommend TM over other meditations in the treatment of high blood pressure. Also, an official of the AHA said that TM had embarrassed the organization by exaggerating study findings on TM for its own commercial purposes.

I continued my response demonstrating the religious character of TM:

Really Bob? What did the New Jersey court say? "Although defendants have submitted well over 1500 pages of briefs, affidavits, and deposition testimony in opposing plaintiffs' motion for summary judgment, defendants have failed to raise the slightest doubt as to the facts or as to the religious nature of the teachings of the Science of Creative Intelligence and the puja. The teaching of the SCI/TM course in New Jersey public high schools violates the establishment clause of the first amendment, and its teaching must be enjoined."

This is what Maharishi himself said about TM mantras in India before coming to the West:

But we do not select the sound at random. We do not select any sound like 'mike', flower table, pen, wail, etc., because such ordinary sounds can do nothing more than merely sharpening the mind; whereas there are some special sounds which have the additional efficacy of producing vibrations whose effects are found to be congenial to our way of life... we do not select any word at random. For our practice, we select only the suitable mantras of personal gods. Such mantras fetch to us the grace of personal gods and make us happier in every walk of life." http://minet.org/www.trancenet.net/secrets/beacon/beacon2.shtml

At some point Roth gets back to religion, but just for a moment:

In the nearly 40 years since the 1979 court case you cite, tens of thousands of students have learned to meditate as part of voluntary Quiet Time programs with the full support of school boards and parents. The results of randomized control trials are very promising and more and better studies are underway. I fully support independent assessments of the impact of Quiet Time using the most stringent research standards. Only then will we really know how good--or not good--it is.

To which I replied:

The age of the court case is not relevant. What is relevant is that TM continues to deceive the public about it's Hindu roots and practices of it's teachers and leadership. How else to explain TM websites hawking Vedic architecture, Hindu astrology, Vedic pundits chanting, yagyas (Hindu prayer services) for sale at astronomical prices.

I also wrote:

> Remember the oath you signed when you became a TM teacher? "It is my fortune, Guru Dev, that I have been accepted to serve the Holy Tradition and spread the Light of God to all those who need it. It is my joy to undertake the responsibility of representing the Holy Tradition in all its purity as it has been given to me by Maharishi and I promise on your altar, Guru Dev, that with all my heart and mind I will always work within the framework of the Organizations founded by Maharishi. And to you, Maharishi, I promise that as a Meditation Guide I will be faithful in all ways to the trust that you have placed in me."

With nothing new to add, Roth circles back to his earlier deflections:

> Just to be clear: Transcendental Meditation is not a religion. Over the past ten years, legal teams from US school boards and governmental agencies have vetted outdated claims (that exist on the internet but not in medical text books) that TM is a religion and have debunked them. TM is offered in hundreds of schools in the US and around the world simply because of science—because it is a simple, non religious, evidence-based technique that reduces stress, improves cognitive function, and promotes health and academic performance. Anything beyond that is simply factually untrue.

Because Roth repeats himself, does that make it true? Is TM really in hundreds of schools? Is it really in those schools simply because of science? If that's true, why does TM go to such lengths to keep secrets about its successes? As will be documented in Chapter 10, TM has an overarching concern with secrecy.[13] They seem to think that those who don't understand the program may cause trouble. Just the opposite is true. The trouble comes from those who understand that TM has no place in public schools.

To summarize, I challenged Mr. Roth on the mantras, the puja, the New Jersey court case that declared TM a religion, and the oath he likely signed pledging his unbounded loyalty to carrying Maharishi's divine mission that is promised on the altar of Maharishi's own guru. TM is science? I don't think so.

Chapter 6

Is TM a Cult?

After reading the first part of this book, you may be wondering if TM is a cult. While writing this book, I've repeatedly asked myself the same question. The answer is complicated because a one-size-fits-all definition of a cult does not exist. Provoking readers to challenge what they have been told about TM is more important to me than any definition.

If you just do TM twice a day for fifteen to twenty minutes, this chapter may strike you as odd because it doesn't reflect your experience, or that of a large majority of people who learn TM. However, having read the last chapter, it should be apparent that TM doesn't involve all members in the same way or influence them all to the same degree. While difficult to state a precise percentage, a subset of TM practitioners seem to possess beliefs and behaviors that, in my opinion, resemble those associated with members of a cultic group. These people bypass the point at which TM is a simple relaxation technique. They are Maharishi's main customers. For them, TM practice increases to as much as three hours, twice a day. They spend many thousands of dollars on advanced TM programs, residence courses, Maharishi-branded elixirs and supplements, as well as recommended Hindu prayer rituals, gemstones, Hindu astrology and architecture. (I was one of them. Fortunately, I left before elixirs, prayer rituals, gemstones, astrology, etc., became standard elements of Maharishi's playbook.)

When the pursuit of enlightenment begins to replace wanting to sleep better or reduce stress, advanced courses and techniques cost more and more money. For some, enlightenment, ever pursued but always elusive and just out of reach, becomes the singular goal around which all life revolves.

Characteristics Associated with Cultic Groups

Researchers have found that various kinds of cults operate similarly with potentially dangerous outcomes. Among the most knowledgeable, Dr. Michael Langone, executive director of the International Cultic Studies Association, has gained a wealth of experience on cult-related topics over the past forty years. His checklist assesses groups, programs, and relationships to determine if the label "cult" applies. It includes social-structural, social-psychological, and interpersonal behavior patterns that are common across cultic environments. As you read this book, decide which, if any, of the points in Langone's checklist are found in TM. The full list is reprinted here with his permission:

- The group displays excessively zealous and unquestioning commitment to its leader and (whether he is alive or dead) regards his belief system, ideology, and practices as the Truth, as law.
- Questioning, doubt, and dissent are discouraged or even punished.
- Mind-altering practices (such as meditation, chanting, speaking in tongues, denunciation sessions, and debilitating work routines) are used in excess and serve to suppress doubts about the group and its leader(s).
- The leadership dictates, sometimes in great detail, how members should think, act, and feel (for example, members must get permission to date, change jobs, marry—or leaders prescribe what types of clothes to wear, where to live, whether or not to have children, how to discipline children, and so forth).

- The group is elitist, claiming a special, exalted status for itself, its leader(s), and its members (for example, the leader is considered the Messiah, a special being, an avatar—or the group and/or the leader is on a special mission to save humanity).
- The group has a polarized us-versus-them mentality, which may cause conflict with the wider society.
- The leader is not accountable to any authorities (unlike, for example, teachers, military commanders or ministers, priests, monks, and rabbis of mainstream religious denominations).
- The group teaches or implies that its supposedly exalted ends justify whatever means it deems necessary. This may result in members participating in behaviors or activities they would have considered reprehensible or unethical before they joined the group.
- The leadership induces feelings of shame and/or guilt in order to influence and/or control members. Often, this is done through peer pressure and subtle forms of persuasion.
- Subservience to the leader or group requires members to cut ties with family and friends, and to radically alter the personal goals and activities they had before they joined the group.
- The group is preoccupied with bringing in new members.
- The group is preoccupied with making money.
- Members are expected to devote inordinate amounts of time to the group and group-related activities.
- Members are encouraged or required to live and/or socialize only with other group members.
- The most loyal members (the "true believers") feel there can be no life outside the context of the group. They believe there is no other way to be and often fear reprisals to themselves or others if they leave (or even consider leaving) the group.[1]

Steven Hassan founded and directs the Freedom of Mind Resource Center in Newton, Massachusetts, and has written several books on cults. In *Combating Cult Mind Control,* he describes "undue influence" on members as a primary feature of cultic groups. He created the BITE model: Behavior, Information, Thought, and Emotional Control. Each overlapping component has an "influence continuum" that identifies characteristics of healthy organizations and unhealthy organizations. On the unhealthy end of the continuum the following traits are listed:

- No informed consent. Information is manipulated and controlled.
- It has a top-down structure, with a single leader at the top and a small inner circle below.
- It is authoritarian: orders are issued from the top.
- It has no guiding ethical principles; all goals justify the use of any means.
- It focuses on controlling, preserving, and acquiring power and information, but shares little of these with rank and file members—and none with outsiders.

For Hassan, cults start with deceptive recruiting (no informed consent), followed by the creation of a cult identity, an identity that is dependent and obedient to an external authority figure who imposes a totalistic doctrine and practice.[2]

Generally, cults lure members in stages. Potential recruits and new initiates often begin by learning a benign philosophy that conceals or downplays the group's main agenda. Only a few at the top know the full story, and they carefully guard the truth through a hierarchy of knowledge and practices. One could argue that many institutions, including recognized religions, operate that way. However, differences exist between an openly religious group that reveals its history and mission versus a secretive organization that pretends to be secular when it is not.

As experienced by Pat Ryan, people may not realize they are part of a cult. Ryan has been a thought reform consultant since 1985, and he founded TM-EX, the first forum for ex-members of TM to share their experiences. He began TM in high school and graduated from Maharishi International University. Ryan attributes many physical and mental symptoms to his TM practice, including what he describes as depersonalization, cognitive distortion, dissociation, confusion, irritability, memory difficulties, and "trance euphoria". However, he did not consider himself in a cult until he joined his family in an intervention to rescue his sister from a cult. Once he learned about cult tactics, he noticed similarities in TM and made the connection.[4] Pat was active in TM for ten years and, upon leaving, almost immediately became an exit counselor; he has helped hundreds of people who believe they have been harmed by TM and other groups for over thirty-five years. He also sued TM for fraud and negligence. TM chose to settle the suit. In recent years, Pat created several websites that target different aspects of cult intervention (see Resource Section).

A former TM teacher (who asked to remain anonymous) sent me his account of what it felt like for him to be in the TM system:

> These organizations and their construction of reality are insidious. They get inside your head. As a true believer, you think you've come to see the light. You may even feel humbled or grateful to have been afforded that opportunity. In doing so, you genuinely believe you've come to your new stand in life on your own, and you're encouraged to believe it. The evidence is clear; the scientific research validates the practice. The possibility of achieving one's full potential, of transcending the mundane shackles of existence lay just ahead.
>
> But the organization's belief systems may be colonizing your mind like an occupying power. You just can't see it. As long as you are in that state of virtual enchantment, you really believe these beliefs are nothing but your own true thoughts.
>
> For the vulnerable, the hook is baited by dangling an enormous prize. If existence is suffused with suffering inside and out, here is a way to end it by rising above. If doubts about life and your place in it trouble you by day and by night, here are

ultimate answers to replace those uncertainties. They seem to offer a way out, a path to traverse. It has its distinctive practices and beliefs, a community, which embraces them, and, not least, an inspired leader who is the source of the wisdom and sole authority.

You come to believe the path leads to a destination, call it enlightenment, sometimes dimly glimpsed, always elusive. The sole purpose is to travel that path and get others to do the same. You give over your life in degrees seeking it. You abandon friends and family. You have new friends and new family. You give up your work to work full-time for the movement.

You practice and you practice, as rigorously and intensely as you can. There is a party line and you try to follow it. You want the express lane to enlightenment, and you travel halfway around the world thinking this time, this course, this will be it.

For a person who values thought, doubts cannot always be eliminated, though. You begin to see that facts are less respected for what they are than the way they can be selectively arranged and presented to make a case, and the case always supports the party line, even though that party line changes over and over. Everything is fodder for marketing, for propaganda.

In the beginning, it's a spiritual regeneration movement. Then, a few years later it's a purely secular scientific-backed practice with no religious or spiritual element at all. As you move into the inner circles, you find out, actually, it's both, and there is no real contradiction. But the masses have to be brought along, and the truth should not be revealed until people are ready for it.

Still later, the ideology of TM as a secular technique lives side-by-side with a heterodox system of Hindu purification rituals, astrology, architecture, medicine, etc. and no one on the inside even seems to think there is a contradiction worth worrying about. And all the while, there is no argument, no conceivable piece of evidence, which could shake the commitment of the true believers. It is a closed system, one that cannot be falsified in the light of experience.

It's simply crazy making. You try to put it aside and 'stay on the program' with unlimited hours of meditation, fasting and many bizarre rituals, as though you are some modern yogi in a cave though in reality, it's a decaying Victorian hotel in Switzerland where you are stuck with a hundred other desperate souls. Then you find that the deeper you get into it the more miserable you feel. They say, just stay with it. You tell yourself you just have to keep at it to break through to the other side. Only there is no other side.

They tell you staying with the program is the only thing that offers any hope at all. As long as you believe that, you keep torturing yourself by doing more of the things that make you feel worse.

And, if, in fact, in some way you have protected a small piece of your authentic self, and it lives on, crouched in a small dark corner of your being and with its independence of judgment, you think, maybe, really, you're right and they're wrong and that this is not the way to be, you face an even deeper dilemma.

You want to believe everything you have swallowed to be true. That's what got you here the first place. To renounce it now, to run away is to do what? It feels like running back to the nothingness that propelled you here in the first place.

So it's agony on top of agony.

As you work to free yourself, at last, you begin to see how insidious it all is, how damaging, and how, in the end, unforgivable.[5]

Maharishi hijacked the concept of enlightenment from the Indian spiritual tradition and radically repurposed it as a tool to recruit and retain converts in his army of missionaries. He not only stripped it from its spiritual source, but he also removed its deep connections to Indian culture and the codes of behavior and moral systems with which they were inextricably entwined. For his followers, he became the sole arbiter of right and wrong.

Attempting to legitimize his actions, Maharishi created a narrative in which he "heroically," but modestly, freed the essential deep wisdom of the Hindu tradition from the cultural trappings and misunderstandings that he said were weighing it down for centuries. In justification, he and his devotees might argue that offering TM to the world was a gift of restoration.

I would argue it was an act of theft, served up with seductively smooth salesmanship and low-key charisma to a naive audience of young, privileged, western youth. What Maharishi lacked in character, he made up for with a combination of brilliant marketing and chutzpah.

Chapter 7

Faulty Research

"There seems to be no study too fragmented, no hypothesis too trivial, no literature too biased or too egotistical, no design too warped, no methodology too bungled, no presentation of results too inaccurate, too obscure, and too contradictory, no analysis too self-serving, no argument too circular, no conclusions too trifling or too unjustified, and no grammar and syntax too offensive for a paper to end up in print."

Dr. Drummond Rennie

Promising Start...Disappointing Results

After celebrity endorsements, "scientific research" is TM's most important marketing tool. Glance at any TM website and you'll see ample confirmation of this statement. This chapter gets somewhat technical, but by analyzing the "science" behind TM, this chapter shows how Maharishi's primary interest in science was selling his products. TM claims to be an effective intervention for many serious problems. In most cases, the supporting documentation for these claims is simply ludicrous.

But before we get into the actual research, I want to highlight a few points that may contribute to the benefits people attribute to TM. First, these people have made a decision to spend time and money on improving their lives. This decision alone can make a positive impact on one's life. Second, because many people are exhausted by their responsibilities and daily routine, if they were to simply take two, twenty-minute naps a day, they would likely feel better. TM essentially allows them to do this (meditating is cool, naps are not). Third is the placebo effect. While not fully understood, it appears that when people believe they are doing something that will make them feel better, they often do.

TM proponents like to point out that TM has received millions of dollars in government grants to study its effectiveness in multiple clinical areas. The statement is true. Twenty-five years ago, TM looked like a promising intervention. TM proponents also like to draw a connection between the total number of research dollars funded and TM's effectiveness. No such connection exists.

Until 2010, TM led the field in funding for meditation studies. During the eighteen years from 1992 to 2010, The National Institutes of Health (NIH) granted a whopping $23 million to Maharishi University. Including the grants awarded before 1992, the total given to Maharishi University to conduct scientific research far exceeds $26 million.

Granting zero dollars between 2010 and 2016, the NIH appears to have stopped giving money to Maharishi University. (Table 1.) The breakdown by individual NIH agencies tells the story; The National Center for Complementary and Alternative Medicine, which gave $7.7 million for TM research from 1999 through 2004, gave nothing after 2004; The National Heart, Blood and Lung Institute, which awarded Maharishi University an astounding $12 million in research grants between 1992 and 2010, gave no money after 2010; and, The National Cancer Institute gave nothing after 1995. Apparently, the NIH's love affair with TM has ended.

Table 1: National Institutes of Health (NIH) Grant Money by Agencies Awarded to Maharishi University (1992 to 2016) *

	NCCAM	NCI	NHBLI	NIA	NIH: all
1992 to 1998	$0	$1,181,324	$1,915,141	$105,900	$5,108,160
1999 to 2004	$7,717,723	$0	$5,432,167	$0	$13,167,444
2005 to 2010	$0	$0	$4,680,981	$0	$4,680,981
2011 to 2016	$0	$0	$0	$0	$0
1992 to 2016	$7,717,723	$1,181,324	$12,028.289	$105,900	$22,956,585

NCCAM = National Center for Complementary and Alternative Medicine; NCI = National Cancer Institute; NHBLI =National Heart, Blood and Lung Institute; NIA = National Institute for Aging.

*Based on information from NIH Research Portfolio Online Reporting Tools (RePORTER)

ClinicalTrials.gov, a repository of information on clinical research studies, is an important gauge of the scientific community's almost complete loss of interest in TM. A review of the number of meditation-related clinical studies listed on the site identifies only fourteen TM studies, and seven of those began in 2001 or earlier.[1]

In contrast, a search on the site using the term "mindfulness" identifies 910 studies currently underway or recently completed by universities and research centers throughout the world.[2] Of these, 190 are specifically focused on Mindfulness-Based Stress Reduction (MBSR) studies, a secular version of mindfulness meditation.[3] The site further identifies 173 "relaxation response" studies underway or recently completed by research centers and universities throughout the world.[4]

There are many reasons for TM's precipitous fall from grace in the research world, including: poorly designed studies that rarely include a randomized active control group, often biased researchers who are affiliated with TM institutions and/or practice TM, and a history of exaggerated findings. In recent years, research has demonstrated that other meditations are as good as TM, if not better, without the religious ceremonies, secret mantras, and the high cost.

Bad Research, Even Worse Results

The Agency for Healthcare Research and Quality (AHRQ), U.S. Department of Health and Human Services, funded a meta-study conducted by the University of Alberta Evidence-Based Practice Center to assess the therapeutic effect of meditation practices on hypertension, cardiovascular diseases, and substance abuse. A meta-study (or meta-analysis) attempts to synthesize research results using various statistical methods to combine and sometimes compare and contrast results from previously separate but related studies. In this study, over eight hundred studies were reviewed, and most of the studies that were included were categorized as poor-quality methodologically, which reflects the state of meditation research in general.

Poor quality data limited the number of comparisons the investigators could complete. However, the comparisons the data did allow reported that, "TM had no advantages over health education to improve measures of systolic blood pressure, diastolic blood pressure, body weight, heart rate, stress, anger, self-efficacy, cholesterol, dietary intake, and level of physical activity in hypertensive patients."[5]

TM: Not A Solution for Psychological Stress

"Meditation Programs for Psychological Stress and Well-Being, A Systematic Review and Meta-analysis," is the published work of researchers at the Johns Hopkins Department of Medicine, who reviewed 18,753 studies on meditation.

Remarkably, only forty-seven studies met the criteria for inclusion, such as random control trials. Of these, only eight TM studies qualified to be included as contrasted to thirty-six mindfulness studies. Mindfulness meditation showed small improvements in a few areas, while other meditation programs, which included TM, had no demonstrably better effect on any of the variables studied than any of the other therapies to which they were compared such as drugs, exercise, and other behavioral therapies.[6]

Meditating and Murder: A Fatally Flawed Crime Reduction Study

In 1995, John Hagelin, a Harvard-trained theoretical physicist, ran

Raja John Hagelin PhD, President, Maharishi University of
Management

as a presidential candidate for TM's Natural Law Party. The centerpiece
of the platform was Maharishi's action plan to revitalize America based
on scientifically proven solutions. Proof would come from an experiment to reduce crime in Washington, D.C., by 20 percent. Supposedly,
the reduction would occur from the coherence achieved when thousands
of TM practitioners meditated together over a fourteen-week period
in Washington, D.C.[7] This came to be known and widely promoted
by TM as "The Maharishi Effect" (supposed brain coherence during
group TM meditation impacting crime).

In his book *Voodoo Science*, Robert Park described a press conference held before the experiment began in which Hagelin explained how
the crime reduction project would be a scientific demonstration that
provided proof of a unified superstring field—an abstract and highly
speculative physical theory that attempts to connect all the forces in
nature. Allegedly, large numbers of advanced TM practitioners meditating together in the same location would access this force, which Hagelin
referred to as "collective consciousness." Thus, as Park reported, medita-

tors serenely went about their practice, and the *Washington Post* made a tally of D.C.'s weekend murders each Monday morning.

The Line Between Foolishness and Fraud

Over the period, the highest murder rate occurred in the city's history. At a press conference held when the study concluded, Hagelin acknowledged that the murder rate had increased, but emphasized that "brutal crime" was down. Noting the absurdity of Hagelin's comment, Park pondered the benefit: "Murderers shot their victims with a clean shot between the eyes rather than bludgeoning them the old-fashioned way!"[8]

The following year, Hagelin returned with a 55-page report on the experiment. At a press conference, he claimed violent crime had dropped 18 percent.[9] One reporter from the *Washington Post* queried, "An 18% reduction compared to what?" Hagelin said the actual crime rate compared to the crime that would have occurred without the meditators meditating. How did he know what the rate would have been? Hagelin answered that by using a "scientifically rigorous time-series analysis that included not only crime data but such factors as weather and fluctuations in Earth's magnetic field." He added that an "independent" scientific review board, several members of which were present at the press conference, had examined the study. Questions from reporters revealed that all the "independent" reviewers were followers of Maharishi.

While Park did not question the sincerity of those involved, he noted, "People will work every bit as hard to fool themselves as to fool others, which makes it very difficult to tell just where the line between foolishness and fraud is located."[10]

According to Peter Woit, a theoretical physicist and senior lecturer in the Mathematics Department at Columbia University, Hagelin's study has since been rejected by "virtually every theoretical physicist in the world" who evaluated it.[11]

Andrew Skolnick, a noted medical writer, wrote, "Indeed, it took Hagelin six years to find a journal willing to publish his much-ridiculed Washington, D.C., crime study. It's not impossible to get flawed and bogus science published in a research journal, it just takes longer."

Perhaps responding to TM's claims that many of its studies appear in "peer reviewed" journals, Skolnick added, "Peer review determines where rather than whether a paper should be published. However, from time to time, 'shoddy science' ends up in the most prestigious of journals."[12]

Pure Fantasy

Why would Hagelin expose himself to such professional ridicule? The answer lies with Maharishi.

Crime reduction was only the start. Maharishi's stated goal was to bring heaven down to earth, although attracting money to TM is likely the more compelling reason. At first, Maharishi claimed that 1 percent of the population had to participate. Aside from lacking any accepted scientific basis whatsoever, the theory's numbers presented an insurmountable problem. In a country like the U.S., for instance, 1 percent of a population of 325,000,000 would have to attract 3,250,000 advanced meditators to meditate together in one place. Maharishi must have quickly realized it would be impossible to attract even a small fraction of that number. In response, he modified the formula. The new formula became the square root of 1 percent of the population. The square root of 3,250,000 is a bit over 1,800; definitely a more realistic number for a country the size of the U.S.

In 2001, a TM insider, also the largest supporter in TM history (he and another family member reportedly donated over $150 million to the movement), considered the tens of millions of dollars that Maharishi was then proposing to spend on large construction projects and airplanes. Instead, the devotee suggested, that to achieve heaven on earth, why not gather ten thousand advanced coherence-generating meditators and have them generate coherence in India. The number was based on an estimated world population of ten billion, which exceeded the actual by a few billion.

Since India would cost a fraction of the Washington, D.C., experiment, this demonstration would be a bargain. Also, the supporter knew for a fact that the funds were readily available to implement the plan.

Maharishi reportedly told his prize benefactor that "[I]f we created the group, then we don't know if it will create world peace or not. We would have to have the group and then see what effect it has."[13]

For decades, Maharishi sold the square root of 1 percent formula to his followers as a fact, not a hypothetical. In the face of Maharishi's shocking admission that he had no idea whether or not the ten thousand meditators would create the desired effect, the supporter understood that the entire scheme had never been anything more than another one of Maharishi's money-making ploys and ended his thirty-year relationship with the guru right then and there.

Unsurprisingly, reputable scientists also concluded the Maharishi Effect was nonsense. In 1986, Heinz Pagels, then executive director of the New York Academy of Sciences, wrote a letter in support of Robert Kropinski, a longtime TM teacher, who had brought a lawsuit against TM for physical, psychological, and financial damage that he attributed to his TM practice. In the letter submitted to the court, Pagels affirmed that the Maharishi Effect accomplished nothing whatsoever, and could be characterized only as a willful deception:

> My summary opinion, as a theoretical physicist specializing in the area of quantum field theory, is that the views expressed in the literature issued by the Maharishi International University, and appearing in the 'World Government News' and other publications associated with the Maharishi Mahesh Yogi that purport to find a connection between the recent ideas of theoretical physics—unified field theory, the vacuum state and collective phenomena—and states of consciousness attained by transcendental meditation are false and profoundly misleading. No qualified physicist that I know would claim to find such a connection without knowingly committing fraud. While I am not an expert on the meditation techniques advocated by the Maharishi, I have experienced and studied meditation methods in the Buddhist and Hindu traditions. There is no known connection between meditation states and states of matter in physics.

Individuals not trained professionally in modern physics could easily come to believe, on the basis of the presentations in the Maharishi literature, that a large number of qualified scientists agree with the purported connection between modern physics and meditation methods. Nothing could be further from the truth.

The notion that what physicists call 'the vacuum state' has anything to do with consciousness is nonsense. The claim that large numbers of people meditating helps reduce crime and war by creating a unified field of consciousness is foolishness of a high order. The presentation of the ideas of modern physics side by side, and apparently supportive of, the ideas of the Maharishi about pure consciousness can only be intended to deceive those who might not know any better.

Reading these materials authorized by the Maharishi causes me distress because I am a man who values the truth. To see the beautiful and profound ideas of modern physics, the labor of generations of scientists, so willfully perverted provokes a feeling of compassion for those who might be taken in by these distortions.[14]

Even Flying Yogis Can't Stop Crime in Fairfield

The population of Fairfield, Iowa, according to the U.S. Census Bureau as of July 2016, was 10,206. Accordingly, applying the square-root-of-one-percent formula, the coherence produced by just ten of TM's coherence producers, the most advanced of which being TM's yogic flyers, should produce a reduced crime rate in the city. For well over two decades, not ten but hundreds of yogic flyers have conducted their coherence-generating practices in the two (male and female) Golden Dome flying centers located on campus at TM's Maharishi University of Management in Fairfield. Also, over a thousand pundits had until recently been chanting Vedic tunes in Maharishi Vedic City, which is just up the road from the campus. The pundits should have exponentially enhanced overall coherence. Based on all the massive level of coherence generated, one might reasonably expect Fairfield to be crime free. In fact, the entire Midwestern U.S. should be crime free. FBI crime statistics tell a different story.

Neighborhood Scout is a real estate platform that analyzes crime rates, schools, and demographic variables in communities in the U.S. Utilizing raw data from the FBI Uniform Crime Reporting Program released in September 2016, Neighborhood Scout reported the following on crime in Fairfield, Iowa:

> **The crime rate in Fairfield is considerably higher than the national average across all communities in America from the largest to the smallest**, although, at 32 crimes per one thousand residents, it is not among the communities with the very highest crime rate. The chance of becoming a victim of either violent or property crime in Fairfield is 1 in 31. Based on FBI crime data, Fairfield is not one of the safest communities in America. **Relative to Iowa, Fairfield has a crime rate that is higher than 94% of the state's cities and towns of all sizes**. (Bold added.)

Also, when comparing Fairfield to other communities of similarly sized populations, Neighborhood Scout found that the Fairfield crime rate (violent and property crimes combined) per thousand residents stood out as higher than most.[15]

Regardless of the fact that causes of crime are many and varied, it is safe to say that the presence of a large number of meditators in Fairfield doesn't appear to be having a crime reducing effect. And, the suicide rate in Iowa also surpassed the national average, according to a 2014 article in a local magazine:

> Since mid-2008, 20 people have died by suicide in the greater Fairfield area, according to the county medical examiner. Four of the deaths have occurred since May of this year. Statewide, suicide rates are on the rise, going from 11.7 to 14.4 cases per 100,000 people from 2010 to 2013, surpassing the national average, according to the American Foundation for Suicide Prevention.[16]

TM and Hypertension: The Hype That Never Dies

TMHome.com makes numerous misstatements about TM and hypertension. As an example, the site features a headline: "TM and healthy, normal blood pressure." Along with identifying behaviors to help maintain healthy blood pressure (diet, exercise, and reducing stress, alcohol, and tobacco), the site makes the following statement: "Luckily, there is a method which is scientifically proven to both reduce stress **and normalize blood pressure – the practice of Transcendental Meditation (TM)."** (Bold added.)[17]

TM has not been demonstrated to normalize blood pressure. Also, the website ignores the most important step in addressing hypertension: seeking competent medical care. Sustained hypertension is a severe, life-threatening medical condition that regularly kills without warning. Leading people to believe that TM alone will normalize the condition could result in serious medical consequences, perhaps even death.

One comprehensive scientific review of alternative approaches to reducing blood pressure by the American Heart Association (AHA), seemingly gives TM sufficient evidence to assert "TM is the only meditation shown to lower blood pressure."[18]

The study, "Beyond Medications and Diet: Alternative Approaches to Lowering Blood Pressure, A Scientific Statement from the American Heart Association," appeared in the April 2013 edition of the journal *Hypertension*. Robert D. Brook, MD of the University of Michigan, chaired a panel of twelve scientists who authored the report:

> Numerous alternative approaches for lowering BP have been evaluated during the past few decades. The strongest evidence supports the effectiveness of using aerobic and/or dynamic resistance exercise for the adjuvant treatment of high BP. Biofeedback techniques, isometric handgrip, and device-guided breathing methods are also likely effective treatments. There is insufficient or inconclusive evidence at the present time to recommend the use of the other techniques reviewed in this scientific statement for the purposes of treating overt hypertension or pre-hypertension.[19]

Note that certain methods—aerobic or dynamic resistance exercise, biofeedback, isometric handgrip, and breathing methods—were found to be most beneficial in *enhancing the effectiveness of medical treatment*.

The authors concluded that while TM and other meditations studied did not appear to be dangerous, more and much higher quality studies were needed to determine what, if any, impact TM had on hypertension:

> The overall evidence supports that **TM modestly lowers BP.** It is **not certain whether it is truly superior to other meditation techniques in terms of BP lowering because there are few head-to-head studies**. As a result of the paucity of data, we are **unable to recommend a specific method of practice when TM is used** for the treatment of high BP. (Bold added.)[20]

The researchers assigned a classification to each modality they reviewed. TM was labeled Level B Class 2B—not a top-notch rating—meaning that TM's usefulness/efficacy was not well established.

The TM organization claimed the study demonstrated TM was better than other meditations investigated in the trial. TM so distorted the study's findings that Matthew Bannister, the AHA's Executive Director of Communications, wrote the following:

"Unfortunately, we have found that some in the media, and many in the TM community, have tried to overstate our findings to promote their own agendas."[21]

Regrettably, some physicians accept TM's exaggerations as fact. One cardiologist appears in a video testimonial for TM on heart health in which she states, "The American Heart Association made a scientific statement that Transcendental Meditation was the only form of stress management and meditation technique to reduce blood pressure. TM is the most efficacious way for us to treat one of the major risk factors of heart disease—stress." As just discussed, the study she references did not make that statement.

The text accompanying the video might lead one to conclude that TM could replace medication—advice that could be dangerous to anyone with sustained high blood pressure. The cardiologist is quoted as telling her patients, "Let's treat blood pressure. Let's treat your cholesterol. Let's treat your stress. And the way we're going to treat these is with Transcendental Meditation practice."[22]

Those who take the time to view the accompanying video will hear her clarify that she recommends TM in conjunction with other medical/pharmaceutical interventions appropriate to the treatment plan she develops for each patient. However, they gain potentially dangerous misinformation when she justifies recommending TM based upon AHA findings: "TM has been proven to reduce heart disease, stroke, and hypertension." The AHA did not state that TM was proven to reduce anything. However, a study of the impact of TM on cardiovascular disease (CVD) reviewed four studies with a total of 430 participants. All were short-term, and there was a risk of bias. The study concluded: "Due to the limited evidence to date, we could draw no conclusions as to the effectiveness of TM for the primary prevention of CVD."[23]

When the American Heart Association's researchers gave TM a mediocre rating, Dr. Robert Schneider was disappointed. As Dean of the College of Maharishi Consciousness-Based Health Care at Maharishi University of Management and Director of the Institute for Natural Medicine and Prevention, Dr. Schneider requested a higher classification for TM in a letter he wrote to Dr. Brook, the study's lead researcher.[24]

Dr. Brook responded with a polite refusal: "TM was not invented to lower BP. We acknowledge that meditation techniques may offer numerous benefits to people. Nevertheless, we believe that existing limitations need to be addressed before revisiting a higher class of recommendation concerning TM for the sole purposes of managing high BP."[25]

Everything That's Wrong with TM Research

Rather than questioning why the rating was low, perhaps a better question could be why it was so high. Of the seven papers that the AHA had reviewed on TM, one with perhaps the strongest positive story for TM was the product of Dr. Schneider and his colleagues: "Stress Reduction in the Secondary Prevention of Cardiovascular Disease: Randomized, Controlled Trial of Transcendental Meditation and Health Education in Blacks."[26]

Larry Husten, a frequent writer for *Forbes*, the editor of cardiology news for CardioExchange (published by the *New England Journal of Medicine*), and the editorial director of WebMD, wrote that on June 27, 2011, only twelve minutes before Schneider's article was to publish in *Archives of Internal Medicine*, the editor of that journal pulled the piece. The decision not to publish was extremely unusual, and Husten investigated.[27]

The next day, Husten reported that while he did not know why the study was pulled, he wrote that those promoting the study were "clearly guilty of gross scientific exaggeration and misstatement." Husten quoted Dr. Norman Rosenthal, a TM advocate who has authored several books on TM, as saying the following on the study, "The prevention of heart attack and stroke and actual lengthening of lifespan by an alternative treatment method is exceedingly rare, if not unprecedented. If Transcendental Meditation were a drug conferring so many benefits, it would be a billion-dollar blockbuster." Not to be outdone, Dr. Schneider pronounced, "These findings are the strongest documented effects yet produced by a mind-body intervention on cardiovascular disease. The effect is as large, or larger than major categories of drug treatment for cardiovascular disease."[28] Upset by Husten's critique, Schneider wrote a thirteen-point defense of the study.[29]

Husten responded to Dr. Schneider by requesting an independent analysis by Sanjay Kaul, M.D., a cardiologist and expert in clinical trials. However, Husten wrote that Kaul's sophisticated analysis wasn't necessary to support his main criticisms:

> Common sense actually works pretty well in this case. A trial with barely 200 patients cannot be expected to provide broad answers about the health benefits of a novel intervention. As Kaul and others have stated on many other occasions, 'Extraordinary claims require extraordinary evidence, and it is quite clear that the evidence in this trial is not extraordinary, at least in any positive sense.'[30]

Moreover, even though no studies had compared the effects of meditation to that of statins, the most widely used pharmacological treatment for elevated high cholesterol, Schneider told WebMD, "What this is saying is that mind-body interventions can have an effect as big as conventional medications, such as statins." In response, Husten wrote that the evidence base for statins is several orders of magnitude greater than for meditation. Also, no study had ever compared meditation and statins. Schneider's comments, Husten said, were preposterous.[31] Referencing the same study, the following statement appears on tm-home.com:

> To see the long-term effects of TM's ability to lower blood pressure, we studied a group of patients with heart disease. Half of them learned TM, half of them served as the control group. We followed them for five years. **Those doing TM had 48% lower rate of heart attack, stroke and death than men and women with similar physical conditions**. (Bold added.)[32]

If the above statement is valid, why aren't medical researchers lining up to replicate the study? Once again, Larry Husten provides the answers:

> Now let's be clear: even if the data from this study turns out to be completely reliable (a point which we can no longer take for granted), the results are at best hypothesis generating and tell us absolutely nothing about the actual value of TM. Only about 200 people were randomized in the study—most studies with hard clinical endpoints require thousands of patients. And a cursory examination of the actual paper raises all sorts of red flags.
> • Although 201 patients are reported in the analysis, the study assessed 451 patients for eligibility and randomized 213 patients.
> • Of the 105 patients randomized to TM, 19 didn't even receive TM.

- 12 patients — 6 in each arm [a treatment group in a clinical trial] — were randomized but then excluded because they did not meet the trial's inclusion criteria.
- 41 patients — 20 in the TM arm, 21 in the control arm — were lost to follow-up.[33]

Husten's next remarks are technical, but important:

But my biggest concern is with the primary endpoint, which was the composite of all-cause mortality, MI [heart attack], or stroke. This occurred in 17 patients in the TM group compared with 23 patients in the control group, a difference that the authors claim achieved significance (p=0.03) *after* adjusting for differences in the age, sex, and use of lipid-lowering drugs between the groups. However, there was no significant difference between the groups in any of these factors. Even worse, there were very significant differences in the amount of education (11.3 years in the TM group versus 9.9 years in the control group, p=0.003) and the CES-D clinical depression scale (13.8 versus 17.7) for which the authors did *not* make an adjustment, although in both cases the imbalance would appear to favor the TM group. **In other words, to use the old cliché, they tortured the data until they made it talk**. (Bold added.)[34]

"For true believers like Schneider," Husten surmised, "fighting heart disease is important only insofar as it can be employed to further the interests of TM. Scientific standards and medical progress are unimportant in the larger scheme of promoting TM."[35] People seeking health remedies cannot be faulted for believing claims that appear to stem from legitimate, respected medical sources like the American Heart Association and highly regarded medical professionals. However, as Husten pointed out, people with real medical issues potentially suffer from highly exaggerated and mischaracterized research.

More Unsubstantiated Claims

TM.org presents TM as the intervention of choice for a variety of high-profile medical and psychological problems. "More evidence-based benefits," is a lead-in for six problems that TM claims to benefit: post-traumatic stress disorder (PTSD), attention-deficit/hyperactivity disorder (ADHD), autism spectrum disorder (ASD), insomnia, depression, and addiction. What evidence does TM present to support its claim as a treatment of choice in addressing these problems? We have to assume what TM presents on TM.org is the best evidence they've got. How strong is the evidence? You are invited to draw your own conclusions.

PTSD

TM.org presents a video under the heading of PTSD that features a soldier for whom TM claims standard treatment had not worked. While the soldier and his wife sit with their eyes closed, a statement appears on the screen stating that they "learned the Transcendental Meditation technique—a stress reducing practice, **proven to combat the effects of PTSD**." (Bold added.)

TM's proof is four studies they present. The first focuses on determining if three soldiers with PTSD could simply learn TM.[36]

The second study reported the effect of TM on Congolese refugees. One must question the relevance of this population to U.S. military personnel. Additionally, the study itself was so compromised, it's worthless. Of 102 study participants (refugees in Kampala, Uganda) who were randomly assigned either to the TM group or a non-matched wait list control group, thirty of the fifty-one participants (59 percent) assigned to the TM group could not attend the meetings. Subsequently, they were dropped, leaving only twenty-one in the TM group. The researchers reported significant reductions in stress from baseline measures that they attributed to TM. One alternate explanation could simply be that the 41 percent of study participants who completed the study had lower stress because they had a somewhat stable living arrangement during the study period than those who dropped out.[37]

The third study was a follow-up of eleven of the Congolese refugees who were still doing TM. That meant that 80 percent of study participants either stopped TM or couldn't be located at follow-up.[38]

The fourth study presented as evidence was an uncontrolled pilot study that taught TM to five veterans with PTSD. Once again, no conclusions on TM and PTSD are possible from such a small sample.[39]

A study with the most relevance on TM and PTSD was just completed at the Veterans Administration San Diego Healthcare System, and is not included on the website. The research compared TM to Cognitive Behavioral Therapy with Prolonged Exposure (CBT-PE) in treating PTSD in war veterans over a three-month period. (CBT-PE is the VA's standard treatment for PTSD.)

The study was categorized as a "non-inferiority" design, meaning the purpose was to determine if TM worked "as well as" the standard behavioral therapy most often used by the VA to treat PTSD. Both TM and CBT produced significantly better results compared to health education classes that served as the control group. There were no significant differences between TM and cognitive behavior therapy. TM wasn't better or worse than CBT, but there were other drawbacks to using TM.

As reported to the author by the lead researcher, some study candidates randomly selected for the TM intervention refused instruction because of what they described as "religious overtones." If all had received full disclosure, the refusal rate might have been significantly higher.[40]

In addition, of the 200 veterans in the study, 67 were randomly assigned to the TM group. The TM organization charged $1,450 per person for instruction, so teaching fees alone added almost $100,000 to the cost of the study. As of September 2014, the number of surviving American veterans who fought in Iraq, Afghanistan, and Vietnam totaled 5.3 million. A conservative estimate of those among them who have PTSD is 750,000.[41] The cost for TM instruction for even a fraction of this group at its current rate of $960 per person would be astronomical.

For all the claims TM makes that it is a cure for PTSD, the best study methodologically shows only that TM appears to be as good as an existing standard treatment used by the VA to treat PTSD.

Another "Scientific" Study: The Power of Suggestion Helps Ten Children with ADHD

TM.org's evidence of TM's effect on ADHD (attention deficit hyperactivity disorder) is an ABC television news report that describes TM as a "solution" for ADHD that "doesn't involve drugs" and "may be able to replace medication." The newscast continues with TM teacher and researcher Dr. Sarina Grosswald describing her study on TM and ADHD. The study had only ten children and was published in an on-line journal. The study was so flawed that it was ridiculed in an article, "How to Design a Positive Study: Meditation for Childhood ADHD":

> The flaws in this study are numerous. The number of subjects is too small, there is no control group and it isn't blinded. The study reveals that some of the children are on medication, but it does not take into account the possibility of recent changes in medical therapy, or improved compliance while on the study. It is based purely on self-report and subjective questionairres [sic] and there is very high liklihood [sic] that a placebo effect could have been the sole responsible factor in the subjects' apparent improvements.[42]

The author saw a video of Grosswald describing her study and further commented:

> A more concerning red flag, and one which was also discovered in the talk given by Grosswald, is the fact that the 10 children involved in the study may have been coached. In the last few minutes of the presentation, Grosswald presents clips of the children meeting with the TM teachers' proponents prior to the initiation of the study, where it appears that they are told what the expected outcome of the trial is, that their symptoms will improve with TM.
>
> Not only are these kids aged 11 to 14 being told what the expected outcome of the study is by study investigators, the headmaster of the school can be seen at the very end of the

video discussing how amazing the technique is and how it will change the students' futures for the better. I am forced to question whether the teachers, whose evaluations of the study subjects' behavior and performance are an integral component of the study conclusions of positive effect, might have been hesitant to give a negative evaluation when their boss is clearly also a true believer.[43]

The ADHD study is so flawed that an important point made in the critique could get lost; one that has particular relevance to any studies of children. The author states that the placebo effect could have been responsible for all of the subjects reported improvements, and it's very easy to understand why. Even before instruction, kids are told over and over again how great TM is and how calming, beneficial and relaxing. And they are going to do better in school as well. Most kids go along with the story because no one wants to be the one who says this isn't working for me. And with TM, the kids are told how special their mantra is—after all, it's so special, you have to keep it a deep secret. It's so powerful and incredibly special that you can't tell anyone. So the table is set, the narrative is locked in, and most people will embrace it—at least for a while. It takes a rare kid, or even an adult, to stand up and say, "No, this isn't working for me."

Science So Bad Even One of Their Own is Furious

One of the comments posted in response to the article was by a TM governor and purusha (TM monk). He stated that he had been practicing TM for thirty-nine years and the TM-Sidha program for decades. He could not contain his disdain for the study:

I'm also an intelligent guy who happens to be a clinical psychologist who knows how to read research. (And my doctorate is not from MERU!) When I see pilot studies like this presented as 'proof' of a causal relationship between TM and shiny bright teeth or whatever it makes me furious. You idiots, do serious research. In this case, ten subjects without a control group? Are you guys nuts? This doesn't mean anything except some sort of weak correlation. I actually use this study in my psychology classes to show what crappy research is. If you believe TM is so robust and has a positive effect on everything, then do good research, not this silly pilot study nonsense.[44]

TM and The Autism Spectrum

The TM.org site shows a video of one mother who discusses how TM has helped her autistic child. That's it—no evidence.

TM and Insomnia: Who Cares What They Really Researched?

TM.org's first evidence of its effect on insomnia has nothing to do with insomnia. It is a letter to a journal from TM researchers complaining that TM wasn't treated fairly in a study.[45]

Likewise, the second study did not mention insomnia. It examined burnout among staff at a school for students with behavioral problems.[46]

The next example presented is a twenty-seven year old study of the health behavior of industrial workers in Japan that appeared in the *Japanese Journal of Public Health*. It was not available online.

Another example of evidence is a thirty-five year old study (also not available online) by a general practitioner in New Zealand. The title of the research, "Transcendental Meditation? Treating the patient as well as the disease," offers no clue that insomnia was even evaluated.[47]

The last study isn't a study at all; it is a talk given by TM's most prolific researcher, David Orme Johnson, who was one of twenty-three speakers at a conference held over twenty years ago.[48]

Don't Have Depression? TM Can Help

TM.org's first example of what it considers evidence for treating depression references a thirty-five year old study and describes it as follows, "Many patients suffering from post-traumatic stress problems who learned the TM technique showed significant reduction in depression after four months, in contrast to others who were randomly assigned to receive psychotherapy." However, only nine veterans were included in the study. So again, the study is too small to learn anything useful about TM and depression other than an attempt by TM to give the impression that "many" patients were helped when there were only nine participants in the entire study.[49]

I could not locate the second study presented when I searched online.[50]

The third study under the depression evidence category involved twenty staff and teachers in a school for students with behavioral problems. If this sounds familiar, it is because TM used the same study to provide evidence of its effect on insomnia. Most importantly, the subjects in this study were not clinically depressed.[51]

The fourth study listed was over forty years old and, again, was not available online.[52]

TM May Have Helped with Addiction, Back in The Good Old Days

Several studies on how TM helps with addiction are listed but the most current is twenty-three years old; two are thirty years old; two are over forty years old. Two reference the same study. The majority of researchers could be considered to be in the TM family and possibly biased.

After 700+ Studies

The over seven hundred studies claimed by TM in the last fifty years have produced more questions than answers:

- Although the TM organization has received at least $25-30 million in government-funded research grants, why have there been so few randomized controlled trials?
- Why are so few TM studies of sufficient quality to allow their inclusion in meta-analysis reviews studies such as the Alberta, University of Michigan, and Johns Hopkins studies?
- Why does virtually no methodologically sound, randomized study include head-to-head comparisons of TM to other meditations—i.e., mindfulness meditation or Benson's Relaxation Response? Almost all of the

few randomized control group studies use "wait list" or "health education classes" as controls.

- What is the likelihood that out of a claimed 700+ studies very few, if any, have reported an adverse finding?

TM has some modestly positive effects, but what has been demonstrated scientifically does not in any reasonable way support the consistently and vastly over-inflated claims made by its proponents. This should make absolutely everyone very cautious when evaluating any claim from the TM organization that TM is good for you.

Chapter 8

The Relaxation Response

What You Can Do Instead of TM

Walter Cannon, a Harvard physiologist, was the first to describe the "fight-or-flight response," a form of self-preservation for mammals in threatening situations. When facing a threat, the body releases certain hormones that increase the heart rate, breath rate, and blood flow. In combination, they produce a heightened physiological state that equips the individual to fight or flee. Fewer people are running from lions and tigers these days, but modern life presents endless triggers that activate the flight-or-fight response. Stress-related illnesses often result when one's sense of well-being and equilibrium are under relentless attack. Stress likely also interferes with the body's healing mechanisms.

Physicians and scientists agree that rest can reduce stress and play a decisive role in restoring and improving overall health. It's little wonder that medical professionals often recommend rest as the main treatment for many illnesses. Following that logic, if rest is used for treating illness, shouldn't deep rest be better?

My friend and fellow student at Berkeley was an emergency room physician. He started practicing TM because he found it helpful in managing his demanding job and graduate studies. I followed his suggestion to try it. I did experience deep rest during my meditation, although I often fell asleep while meditating and attributed part of my experience of deep rest to sleep. Nevertheless, I saw a potentially significant role for TM in preventive medicine because I understood that deep rest would have a positive impact on many stress related illnesses. At the time, TM was the only way I knew to achieve that level of rest.

Maharishi Missed the Point

Dr. Herbert Benson, a Harvard researcher, coined the term the "Relaxation Response." While Maharishi's focus was on higher consciousness, Dr. Benson was focused on health. His primary interest in the mind settling down was the effect that settling down had on the body; if meditation could allow the physiology to experience very deep rest, it could potentially play a role in improving health. Benson agreed to include TM in his studies. Benson and Keith Wallace studied TM practitioners and measured significant reductions in heart rate, metabolic rate, and breath rate during their TM practice. They labeled the combination of changes, "a wakeful hypo metabolic physiologic state," which Benson later called the Relaxation Response. Benson hypothesized that a rested body could play a significant role in the treatment of medical problems in which stress was either a primary or a contributing factor and devoted his career to researching this topic. He is a pioneer in the field of mind-body medicine.[1]

However, a big problem soon developed for TM. Dr. Benson was a scientist and did not practice TM. Maharishi wasn't his guru. As such, he tested another hypothesis: Could other methods elicit the Relaxation Response as well as TM? Borrowing from TM, Benson identified what he initially thought were four critical components to elicit the Relaxation Response:

- A quiet environment
- A mental device—a sound, word, phrase, or prayer, repeated silently or aloud, or a fixed gaze at an object
- A passive attitude—no worrying about how well one is performing the technique; innocently putting aside any distracting thought to return to one's focus

- A comfortable position

At a later point, Dr. Benson concluded that a mental device and a passive attitude were the only essential factors. Quiet wasn't necessary. A person could meditate anywhere. (I practiced TM on planes, trains, and buses). Benson also realized that a comfortable position wasn't necessary. A person could trigger the Relaxation Response while jogging, walking, rowing a boat, or knitting. The requirements were simple: repeating a mental device (the chosen word or sound), and maintaining a passive attitude towards intruding thoughts. When thoughts were noticed, one easily returns to the chosen word or sound.

Most importantly, Benson demonstrated that the centerpiece of TM—the mantra—was unnecessary. Maharishi had said that any sound would work to settle the mind. Ironically, Benson's research proved Maharishi correct. Initially, Benson found repeating the word "one" elicited the Relaxation Response. Later he demonstrated that virtually any word or short phrase could do the same. Once a consistent method of eliciting the Relaxation Response was confirmed, Benson and his colleagues turned their attention to demonstrating its effectiveness in treating a wide range of medical conditions.[2]

Potential Impact on Health Care Utilization

In recent years, growing numbers of healthcare providers have documented that deep rest can beneficially influence the prevention and treatment of many stress-related illnesses. Countries like the United States face out-of-control medical costs that are compounded by an aging population that requires more care. Inexpensive treatments that help improve one's health and result in fewer medical visits, treatments, and procedures are critically needed. A relaxation technology that meets certain criteria should receive widespread acceptance when complementing medical treatment. At a minimum, these criteria include:

- It should be widely available and taught in a uniformly consistent manner.
- It should be easy for medical and mental healthcare

providers to learn to teach.
- It should be easy to learn.
- It should be inexpensive.
- A body of quality, independent research should support it.
- It should be free of religious/spiritual trappings.

Benson's Relaxation Response meets all the above criteria.

Enemy of the Movement

When I began working at the National TM Center in Los Angeles, Dr. Benson, early in his career at Harvard, was regarded as a movement hero. While virtually all health-conscious people today understand that the mind and body are connected, medical professionals once considered the concept radical. TM was considered a counterculture practice, and those who had even heard of Maharishi knew him as the guru who befriended The Beatles. Against this backdrop, when Dr. Benson agreed to study TM's effect on physiology, he was risking his position at Harvard.

But in 1975, Dr. Benson went from the TM movement's greatest hero to its greatest enemy. All these years later, I can still remember feeling that the scientist had made a huge mistake, and most everyone in TM agreed. Benson claimed his Relaxation Response was as effective as TM in producing the deep rest that was at the heart of its ability to impact illness. We didn't believe it. How could the word "one" possibly be as effective as the TM mantras that, as Maharishi declared, only had "life- supporting effects"? How could "one" be life-supporting? Many of us thought it might actually be dangerous. TM's introductory lectures no longer mentioned Dr. Benson. In the TM world, Dr. Benson ceased to exist.

TM proponents claim that it is superior to the Relaxation Response. While TM has received close to $30 million in research grants (certainly enough money to fund at least one methodologically sound head-to-head comparison of the two practices), they have chosen not to do that study.

The Relaxation Response has clear advantages over TM. It is easy to learn without introductory lectures, four days of instruction, or the secretive religious or guru trappings. It doesn't cost almost $1,000 for the entry-level course. You can learn it from a book or take advantage of inexpensive instructional CDs available online.[3]

By the year 2000, Dr. Benson's first book, *The Relaxation Response*, had been translated into thirteen languages and had sold over four million copies. It was the number one self-help book for several years following its initial publication. He and his colleagues (in what is now The Benson-Henry Institute for Mind Body Medicine at Massachusetts General Hospital) have treated thousands of patients and published scores of studies in medical and other professional journals demonstrating that the Relaxation Response has a major role in improving many medical issues, including:

- angina pectoris
- cardiac arrhythmias
- allergic skin reactions
- mild and moderate depression
- bronchial asthma
- herpes simplex (cold sores)
- cough
- constipation
- diabetes mellitus
- duodenal ulcers
- dizziness
- fatigue
- hypertension
- infertility
- insomnia
- nausea and vomiting during pregnancy
- pain (backaches, headaches, abdominal pain, muscle pain, joint aches, postoperative pain, neck, arm and leg pain)
- postoperative swelling

- premenstrual syndrome
- rheumatoid arthritis
- side effects of cancer
- side effects of AIDS[4]

While believing that every illness has a mind-body component, Dr. Benson doesn't claim that the Relaxation Response is a cure for every medical problem. And, unlike TM, he requires that addressing any medical problem begins with a complete medical evaluation and that treatment consider every available tool (including prescription drugs and surgery, if indicated).

With a healthy measure of a scientist's curiosity, Dr. Benson wanted to measure how advanced meditation practices affected physiology. In the twenty-fifth anniversary edition of *The Relaxation Response*, he wrote that his friendship with the Dalai Lama paved the way for the scientist and his team to make repeated trips to Northern India. They brought scientific measuring equipment to study Tibetan monks living there in exile.

At an elevation of 15,000 feet in the Himalayas, they watched as scantily clad monks, draped in wet sheets, meditated and raised their body temperature so that their bodies produced steam and dried the wet sheets within minutes. The monks had added one step beyond the usual Relaxation Response: They visualized a fire or heat that they could channel through an imagined central vessel of their body.[5]

In his second book, *Beyond the Relaxation Response*, Dr. Benson added another component that increased the effectiveness of the Relaxation Response: the power of belief, or what he called "the faith factor." He found that the benefits of the Relaxation Response could be enhanced when combined with a deeply held set of philosophical or religious convictions. A religious or more spiritual person who used a word or short prayer from his or her faith achieved better results with the Relaxation Response and, on average, continued the practice longer.[6]

While the addition of belief possibly opened another self-healing channel, Dr. Benson also found that belief did not have to be religious. People who reported that they believed in the healing power of their body also enhanced the effectiveness of the Relaxation Response. Accordingly, while any word used correctly would elicit the Relaxation Response, a word that had significance to the person or even a belief in the body's ability to heal accelerated the healing process.

In *Relaxation Revolution*, Benson's later book, he included a chapter on creating a personalized plan to address specific medical problems that included two phases. In phase one, the Relaxation Response is elicited for an average of twelve to fifteen minutes daily for a minimum of eight weeks. Many achieve the desired health outcome with the first phase. Phase two, if required, involves eight to ten minutes of visualization immediately following the Relaxation Response phase. In the visualization step, one brings to mind calming, soothing memories or other pleasant imagery. According to the theory, the relaxed mind is more open to a visualization process. For example, a person might visualize being free of pain. Dr. Benson further used a technique he termed "remembered wellness" to describe a visualization process during which a patient recalls a state of wellness enjoyed in the past. The working hypothesis is that remembered wellness can counteract remembered illness, which, over time, loosens its grip on the person.[7]

The Benson-Henry Institute for Mind Body Medicine at Massachusetts General Hospital (BHI) has published over one hundred studies on the Relaxation Response and its application in both the prevention and treatment of stress-related illnesses. Most of the studies were published in respected journals, and many of the scientists are on staff at some of the world's best research institutions, including Harvard University and Massachusetts General Hospital. The research tremendously benefits from BHI being an integral component of Mass General and having a research staff closely involved with and often providing patient care.[8]

Most Significant Study from a Public Health Perspective

One retrospective study examined the effects of the Relaxation Response Resiliency Program (3RP) on medical care utilization. 3RP is an enhanced Relaxation Response program targeting patients with chronic stress, who agreed to three individual appointments and eight weeks of two-hour group sessions as part of their treatment. In addition to Relaxation Response training, participants received education on the role of stress and physical/emotional problems, the power of thinking positively, the importance of belief, the role of a healthy diet, sufficient sleep, and physical activity.

The study compared 4,452 patients who had received 3RP training at BHI for over eight years (from January 2006 to July 2014) to a control group of 13,149 who had not received the 3RP training. All study participants were members of a major U.S. academic health network for a median period of 4.2 years. 3RP's impact on medical care utilization was extraordinary:

- Total utilization decreased by 43%
- Clinical encounters decreased by 41.9%
- Imaging decreased by 50.3%
- Lab encounters decreased by 43.5%
- Medical procedures decreased by 21.4%[9]

Widespread utilization of the Relaxation Response presents a tremendous opportunity for health care in America. Unless something changes, those with financial resources will continue to have access to some of the best medical care in the world, while those without resources will have far more limited choices.

Recognition of the mind-body connection from the established medical community has made enormous strides. However, more needs to be done. Complete acceptance will require proof from large-scale studies of the Relaxation Response on medical care utilization. If further research demonstrates even a fraction of the reductions in utilization, as reported in the 3RP study, out of control healthcare expenditures could be slashed.

Training and Certification

Relaxation Response training for medical and mental health practitioners is already available through BHI. The Institute offers the Stress Management and Resiliency Training (SMART) program allowing licensed healthcare professionals to earn certification and teach the program to their clients. Currently, plans are underway to open training to a wider user base, including teachers. A full description of the certification program is currently available online.[10]

The following characteristics of the SMART certification program have great merit:

- It allows healthcare practitioners to offer their patients a simple, easily learned, inexpensive technique to reduce the debilitating effects of stress in their lives.
- It gives health maintenance organizations and health networks the option of providing Relaxation Response training to their members, which will likely result in lower costs and a better quality of life for their members.

Decades of research on the Relaxation Response demonstrate that healthcare providers can confidently recommend the technique to their patients for a wide variety of clinical issues. Patients can be guided to learn the practice themselves from inexpensive teaching materials available through the Benson-Henry Institute. Larger practices, clinics, and hospitals could designate a staff member (or members) to receive SMART training and teach the Relaxation Response on site.

Chapter 9

Is Meditation for Everyone?

Genetic advantages and cultural influences equip some people to withstand stress better than others, but no one escapes unscathed. It's little wonder, then, that so many who are searching for a way to relax turn to meditation, hoping it will give them peace of mind.

The ability to deeply relax by retreating to a quiet space within oneself can be beneficial. This experience over time can have strengthening effects on overall physical and mental health. However, if you feel good about yourself and your situation, there may be no need to meditate. You may have better things to do with the time that meditation requires. Also, although infrequent, side effects are possible.

Writing this book and having been a TM teacher for over ten years did not made me an expert in meditation. If anything, my research has given me an appreciation of how little I knew about meditations other than TM. It has also allowed me to appreciate the very significant role that the Relaxation Response and mindfulness meditation have been demonstrated to play in a number of clinical applications. Of course, the research existed; I just wasn't aware of it. Finally, I believe that I have gained a few, mostly common-sense insights about meditation that may be helpful to some.

Replace a TM (or Any) Mantra with a New One

If you already have a TM mantra and you are uncomfortable with the mantra/deity issue, you may want to consider changing it. Changing your mantra is not hard and will likely work just as well as the TM mantra you were given. If you think your TM mantra is unique, remember that your age (and possibly your sex) at the time you learned TM was the only criteria in its selection, and that Maharishi changed these categories several times over the years[1]. So much for any special sanctity of your TM mantra.

To change your mantra, pick a sound that you like or a word that has a special meaning to you. If you prefer, choose a word or short phrase from your religious tradition and use it instead of your TM mantra. Most likely, the TM mantra will continue to pop up because you are used to it. Don't fight it. Treat it like any other thought. That means that when you realize you're thinking your old mantra, easily return to your new one. Don't expect to get rid of your TM mantra overnight; the change will happen over time.

Treating the Unknown Too Lightly

In general, people don't know very much about meditation. Although Western society treats it lightly, meditation has always been central to a spiritual path of almost every religion. The effects of meditation can be powerful. That power doesn't diminish because most people in Western countries primarily use meditation to deal with stress or to relax.

When a person meditates, and the mind begins to settle down, the possibility of accessing some rough patches in one's psyche is significant. At times, meditation can trigger painful, perhaps repressed, memories that might be extremely traumatic to experience—or re-experience. This triggering is a possibility for any trauma that remains emotionally unprocessed. If suppressed memories that, by definition, are too painful to remember consciously surface during meditation, help may be necessary to process them. Without support, the meditation experience could do more harm than good. It is common sense that someone with PTSD or a history of psychiatric problems should meditate with appropriate supervision that might allow traumatic, repressed issues to be resolved.

Meditation is not for everyone, but if you decide to meditate, choosing the right meditation is important. In addition, there are steps you can take to minimize the risk of harmful side effects.

Start slowly and only meditate as long as it feels comfortable. Don't go beyond twenty minutes each time or more frequently than twice a day. The majority of people who got in trouble with TM were meditating more often and for longer periods of time during each session.

If the meditation experience is uncomfortable, stop meditating. You might consider trying again a day or two later. If the discomfort persists, you might want to consider another way to relax. While this recommendation likely seems like common sense, when I became a TM teacher, the guidelines I was given recommended continuing TM even in the face of pain or shaking that the meditator might be experiencing during, and even after meditation. The belief was that fixing the meditation would fix the problem. Unfortunately, it didn't always work that way.

Mindfulness Meditation

Jon Kabat-Zinn, Professor of Medicine Emeritus and founder of the Stress Reduction Center at the University of Massachusetts Medical School, originated Mindfulness Based Stress Reduction (MBSR). He defined mindfulness as paying attention in a certain way: on purpose, in the present moment, and nonjudgmentally.[2] Kabat-Zinn was inspired by his experience with Zen Buddhism and its practices and philosophy in which mindfulness plays an important role. He developed MBSR in the 1970s as a secularized version of mindfulness and said that MBSR is not Buddhism and that he did not want it tied to any particular religious belief.

While "mindfulness meditation" may be useful in addressing certain medical or mental health problems, a recent study has highlighted a number of issues demonstrating methodological weaknesses in most mindfulness studies. The author's point out that the methodological weaknesses in past studies could lead to harming, misleading and disappointing results for those who start. And they also describe a lack of consensus regarding even definitions of mindfulness that makes measuring its effects extremely challenging.[3]

Regardless of these challenges, mindfulness is extremely popular as a way to relax and increase awareness. In recent years, it has also been found to be effective in a number of clinical areas. However, more research is necessary to define just how useful and in what clinical applications.

Like TM, mindfulness is vulnerable to exaggerated claims. But unlike TM, there are serious people trying to walk the exaggerations back. *Altered Traits: Science Reveals How Meditation Changes your Mind, Brain and Body*, by Daniel Goleman and Richard Davidson is a recently published comprehensive review of the improving state of meditation research by two of the top leaders in the field. It reports on where mindfulness seems to work and where it doesn't.[4]

They point out that even if meditation isn't clinically better for certain problems than existing treatments, including therapy or medication, it may still be better than either one. For example, soldiers with PTSD often resist talk therapy and many hate the side effects of medications used to treat PTSD. Many refuse or sabotage therapy and often don't take their medication. In these instances, meditation, even without being more effective than existing treatments, may still be the better choice.

Of particular promise is a movement among psychotherapists to blend mindfulness-based meditation with cognitive therapy (MBCT). The author's point to over 1,100 articles combining mindfulness with cognitive therapy, with 80 percent of them published in the last five years.

> This integration continues to have a wide impact in the clinical world, with empirical tests of applications to an ever larger range of psychological disorders under way. While there are occasional reports of negative effects of meditation, the findings to date underscore the potential promise of meditation-based strategies, and the enormous increase in scientific research in these areas bodes well for the future.[5]

Another recent study of Buddhist meditation practitioners and experts identified a range of experiences described as challenging, difficult, and distressing. While many study participants reported positive experiences, some reported negative experiences that ranged from minimal and transient to severe and enduring.[6] Many of the problems occurred during or shortly after longer meditation sessions at meditation retreats. Limiting the meditation time to fifteen to twenty minutes twice a day and stopping if problems occur should mitigate many of the challenges described in this study.

People with mental health or addiction problems should be cautious about starting to meditate on their own. Fortunately, as mentioned above, many therapists are using meditation in their practices along with other treatments, with much-reported success. Ideally, those with significant mental health or addiction problems would choose a therapist who incorporates meditation in their treatment plans and who could select the best meditation for the individual and guide or intervene as necessary. The therapist would be responsible for adjusting the time and frequency of the meditation as indicated by the patient's progress (or lack thereof). Meditation sessions should be modified to suit the patient just like any other treatment modality or medication for that matter. Moreover, meditation is not necessarily a lifetime practice, and continuing to meditate should be reevaluated when symptoms diminish or stop.

With the above caveats, meditation may be useful as an adjunct to therapy, and should be more widely available. One way to accomplish this is for mental health associations to encourage their members to train to use meditation in their practices, and efforts should be made to publicize the availability of trained practitioners in the broadest possible manner.

Meditation Resources

There are a number of secular meditations available free or at minimal cost. They include Benson's Relaxation Response and mindfulness meditation.

The Benson-Henry Institute for Mind Body Medicine at Massachusetts General Hospital (BHI)

BHI is dedicated to research, teaching, and clinical applications to treat and prevent stress-related illnesses. The Relaxation Response is the cornerstone of its treatment plans. The BHI training programs offer the ability to teach the Relaxation Response systematically in medical and mental health practices, as well as in schools, at a fraction of the cost of TM. The BHI website offers guided meditations on CDs and DVDs that can be purchased to learn the technique:

https://www.bensonhenryinstitute.org/meditation-cd-and-dvd/

Mindfulness Meditation Resources

There are many MBSR meditation resources on the web. However, some Buddhist influences do appear in some of them to a greater or lesser degree. If this is a concern, they are easy to avoid. For example, some guided meditation videos have a religious statue in the background. If this is a concern, one can listen to the videos rather than watch them. Some meditations begin and end with cymbals, bells, chimes, or singing bowls, all of which are at times found in Buddhist meditation. If desired, the traditional notifications can be avoided with gentle alarms or vocal instructions to begin and end the meditation.

Mindful Awareness Research Center at UCLA (MARC)

MARC's primary focus is mindful awareness and bringing mindfulness into one's life. It offers a comprehensive training program in mindfulness meditation, as well as a weekly drop-in, thirty-minute guided meditation at UCLA's Hammer Museum. Free mindfulness podcasts are available on iTunes.

http://marc.ucla.edu/about-marc

Calm.com

Calm.com offers hundreds of online meditations that run the gamut of mindfulness meditations, including relaxation, breathing exercises, and sleep exercises. Meditations are available on a subscription basis, currently $60 per year or $300 for lifetime access.

Headspace.com

Headspace is an online mindfulness meditation site that includes hundreds of themed sessions on everything from stress to sleep. There are meditations for children, short meditations for busy schedules, and even SOS exercises in case of sudden meltdowns. Major categories include relationships, motivation, anxiety, and focus. There is a free trial available, and an annual subscription is currently $96.

Noga Sound Solutions

This is a selection of twelve brief audios to enhance daily life through practicing simple exercises and techniques. These recordings employ the spoken voice and nature sounds, as well as binaural beat technology (designed to put your brain into the same state as when you are meditating). The tracks are either relaxation (such as visualization, slow breathing, etc.) or meditation techniques (such as mindful focus on the breath). The series is available for $25 Download or $30 CD. https://store.cdbaby.com/cd/darcyrdwallen2

Transform Your Life – Health Based Meditation Program

This is a series of fourteen health-based meditations by therapists who use meditation and relaxation techniques in their practices. The series is available on iTunes for $30.

https://itunes.apple.com/us/artist/mordechai-chemel/id550434952

Chapter 10

TM in Public Schools and the Quest for Government Funding

A Culture of Deception

Why does TM go to such lengths to deny its spiritual/religious essence?

At least part of the denial is motivated by TM's effort to gain acceptance in public schools. Currently, TM instructional and program costs in public schools are primarily funded through contributions to the David Lynch Foundation. But the brass ring has always been government funding that TM ultimately hopes will pay for hundreds of thousands, if not millions, of students. That means that TM has to keep its Hindu underpinnings out of public sight.

A few years ago, TM teacher George Hammond rocked the TM organization when he claimed that, in a lengthy meeting, Maharishi had given him a message to share with TM leaders. Maharishi, it seemed, had a few concerns about how the organization was running and a few suggestions to improve the situation. Hammond tried to get a meeting with TM's leaders, but they weren't interested. I imagine there might have been some concern because when George and Maharishi met, Maharishi had already been dead for over five years.

When Hammond couldn't get the meeting, he issued an open invitation to a presentation he would make in an auditorium that would also be live-streamed on the Internet. Raja John Hagelin realized Hammond could create a public relations disaster for TM. But while he couldn't kill Hammond's performance, he tried to minimize its impact; he instructed all certified governors to ignore the event. Primarily, he feared that the presentation could jeopardize TM's efforts to get government and corporate funding for its programs. In an email to certified governors, Hagelin wrote:

> We have seen wonderful, growing support from government, public education, business, the Pentagon, the VA, and the educated public. To suddenly create the public impression that the Movement is now based on séance, on channeling the departed, or on the hearsay of any individual who is acting entirely on his own…the press would have a field day, potentially turning Maharishi's entire Movement into a laughing stock. **It could undermine our very delicate programs in public schools, the military, the VA, the NIH, with businesses and serious people everywhere**. (Bold added.)[1]

Why, in Hagelin's words, are TM's programs in public schools "very delicate"? Because, TM can't reveal its Hindu practices without risking challenges by parents, most of whom probably wouldn't want their children exposed to TM's secret initiations and mantras if they knew what they were. They might also be concerned if they knew (as documented later in this chapter) that TM was thrown out of the New Jersey schools because the New Jersey court ruled TM embodied religious practices that were prohibited by the U.S. Constitution. So TM is forced to present itself as a secular, scientific technique. With meditation and yoga so popular in the U.S., the organization has positioned itself as a valid choice to achieve the perceived benefits of meditation. The stakes couldn't be higher. In addition to potentially huge cash infusions, TM is counting on the next generation of young recruits to support the organization. Success depends on TM not looking too weird or religious in mainstream America's eyes. TM's problem is that it is both.

David Bardin, an attorney who has represented anti-cult groups, wrote an article for the International Cultic Studies Association that appeared on the association's website. Bardin included the following quote from *Heaven on Earth, Dispatches from America's Spiritual Frontier* (Crown 1992), an investigative report on New Age culture written by Pulitzer Prize-winner, Michael D'Antonio:

> I would have welcomed the discovery of a middle way, a path to spirituality that was consistent with reason. But TM, as it is practiced at MIU, isn't a middle ground. For the first time in my travels through New Age America, I worried that I was observing a cult rather than a culture. MIU and the Maharishi would take control of everything — right down to matters of food, shelter, and child rearing — for the most devout.
>
> [TM'ers] have accepted rigid, authoritarian control in exchange for security. Far from being a place where individuals grow and innovate, the Fairfield TM community is regimented and constricted. All conflict, doubt, perhaps even all genuine emotion, is stifled and covered over with a pleasant veneer.[2]

When we understand the true nature of the TM organization, some critical issues arise regarding its current push to mainstream in our public schools. First, our children are our most precious resource; they are also vulnerable and impressionable. Are we not obligated to protect them from any group that pretends to be something it is not?

Don't Let TM Near Your Kids

Initially, when talking to Hindus in India in 1955, and a few years later in July 1959, when he created his first organization in the U.S., the Spiritual Regeneration Movement (SRM), Maharishi was open about TM's spiritual goals. The only problem was that it was too early to sell Eastern spirituality in America. The spiritual seekers, propelled by the hippie movement and The Beatles, who gave Maharishi a spotlight on the world stage, would come years later.

Perhaps as an accommodation to the reality of the marketplace, Maharishi made some strategic changes in the early 1970s. He downplayed spirituality. Now that Eastern philosophies are widely accepted in Western culture today, why continue the charade? I believe it is because they hope that journalists, school administrators, school board members, and even school attorneys (who should know better) won't dig below the surface and will accept whatever TM proponents tell them at face value. They may hope that the cost of lawsuits to challenge TM in public schools will be too expensive and time-consuming to pursue. And while the stakes are high for TM, they are much higher for our children.

San Francisco Public Schools: A Case Study

San Francisco School Superintendent, [...] a reputed TM practitioner, who saw nothing wrong with our children bowing and making offerings to an altar, in a darkened room in isolation from their peers, or with our children being told to keep a secret from their parents by a comparative stranger, will be moving to the Houston School District. Let us hope he will not bring his 'active promotion' of such practices with him to Texas.

Parents Against TM in Public Schools.
Facebook. Retrieved July 27, 2016.

A parent, who felt isolated in her struggle against the intrusion of TM in her child's school, launched SF Parents Against TM in Public Schools on Facebook to express her frustrations. While other parents joined the discussion, the school district remained silent.

The mother first learned that her son was selected for TM instruction in his San Francisco public school when he brought home a permission slip that would allow him to participate. The form was only printed in English, which she thought unusual, as the school always issued a Spanish translation of any parent communications to reach the large Hispanic parent population. As an active, high school parent, she was also surprised that she'd heard nothing about the program in advance.

The form stated that TM was scientifically proven, not religious, and a program with many benefits. It had *no* opt-out portion. Since her son said he wanted to participate to earn school credit, the mom signed the agreement.

Not long after, her son informed her that his classmates were leaving the classroom, a few students at a time, to meet with an "instructor." The mom, realizing the individual was a TM teacher, was deeply concerned about her son and other students leaving their class with someone she had neither met nor was an official school employee. Thus, the instructor was not bound by the same ethical standards as credentialed educators. Immediately, she emailed her son's health class teacher, who was also the liaison to the TM program at the school and copied the school's principal. In the email, she rescinded permission for her son to participate in the TM program and further instructed that he was not to be allowed to interact with any TM staff connected to the program.

The incident prompted the mom to research TM online. She reported scrolling through an abundance of TM advertisements and links to pro TM articles before encountering any negative articles, including information about mantras and pujas. As a former practicing Hindu, she immediately recognized the mantras as names of Hindu deities.

Meanwhile, the mother received an invitation to meet with the school principal. At the meeting, she asked the principal how she could not be concerned that TM had religious overtones. She felt obliged to coach her on the First Amendment's requirement of the separation of church and state. The principal had been instructed in TM and experienced the puja; however, when pressed, the mother reported she replied, "But they told us it wasn't religious."

After that meeting, she received a "cease and desist" letter from someone she considered "an expensive lawyer from a large office specializing in political campaigns," alleging that she was "apparently" accusing the TM program personnel of trying to spread religion in her son's school. Feeling the need to protect herself, the mom obtained legal representation, and her attorney responded to the letter. So far TM has left her alone. How troubling is it that a parent of a minor would believe she required legal representation for describing firsthand facts and concerns about a program in her child's public school?

According to the mother, TM had been in six San Francisco schools:

Wallenberg High School, Sala Burton High School, Thurgood Marshall High School, Visitation Valley Middle School, John O'Connell High School, and Everett Middle School. Whether by coincidence or design, all participating schools are in low-income communities with many non-English-speaking parents.

A TM advocate might argue that the need was greatest in those neighborhoods, but a skeptic might argue that minority parents in low-income schools would be less likely to question authority. Skeptics might also suggest that targeting low-income schools generates positive publicity for TM and inspires benefactors who believe they are doing good work by helping low-income kids.

According to the above-mentioned mother, five of the six schools have dropped the TM program. Visitation Valley Middle School is the only school that still has the Quiet Time program. It is funded by the David Lynch Foundation.

She further reported that the TM program, "altars and all," was booted from her son's high school after about three months. Without knowing what prompted faculty decisions, she learned that only two of approximately thirty high school staff members had voted to keep it. The David Lynch Foundation did not pay for the TM instruction at her son's school. She reported that the taxpayer cost of three months of TM at the school was $111,000. I was able to verify this amount independently.

TM's honeymoon in San Francisco could be approaching an end with "mindfulness meditation" under consideration as an alternative. The same mom, in fact, has learned that workshops for training in non-TM meditations have been taking place at her son's school.

A goal of this book is to empower concerned citizens, particularly parents, to confront and expose TM's deceptions and secrets. Unfortunately, TM's slick marketing has misdirected many teachers and administrators who have the best intentions for their students. Intentions are not the issue. The welfare of children is what matters.

TM Tossed from Public Schools

In *Malnak v. Yogi* (592 F.2d 197), a New Jersey court ruled that a curriculum in the Science of Creative Intelligence (SCI), which is the philosophic underpinning of the TM technique, could not be taught in New Jersey's public schools. The decision rested on a comparison of the TM SCI's teachings and Hinduism, and further noted that the puja chant "is an invocation of a deified human being who has been dead for almost a quarter of a century."

As such, the court ruled that TM in public schools violated the Establishment Clause of the First Amendment, which created a wall of separation between church and state. The lower court based its ruling, in part, on the religious puja ceremony involved in TM instruction and on the fact that TM's Westernized philosophy, the Science of Creative Intelligence, dealt with issues of ultimate concern, truth, and other ideas analogous to those in well-recognized religions. The court could not have been clearer in its ruling against TM:

> Although defendants have submitted well over 1500 pages of briefs, affidavits, and deposition testimony in opposing plaintiffs' motion for summary judgment, **defendants have failed to raise the slightest doubt as to the facts or as to the religious nature of the teachings of the Science of Creative Intelligence and the puja.** The teaching of the SCI/TM course in New Jersey public high schools violates the establishment clause of the first amendment, and its teaching must be enjoined. (Bold added.)[3]

With so much at stake, TM appealed the New Jersey decision taking the position that the district court had erred in determining that the Science of Creative Intelligence/Transcendental Meditation constituted an "establishment of religion" in violation of the First Amendment of the U.S. Constitution. The United States Court of Appeals, Third Circuit, denied the appeal and, on February 2, 1979, affirming the lower court decision.[4]

Putting the First Amendment issue aside, parents should be very concerned about exposing their children to an organization led by individuals who function within a fantasy world they call the Global

Country of World Peace (GCWP). In 2000, Tony Nader M.D., Ph.D., was appointed the First Sovereign Ruler of GCWP. Following Maharishi's death in 2008, Nader took over the movement and took the title *His Majesty Maharaja Adhiraj Raja Raam*. The coronation reportedly entailed a five-day affair in TM's 200-room world headquarters in Vlodrop, Holland.[5]

David Wants to Fly, a compelling 2010 documentary by David Sieveking, captures TM's fantasy world and a disturbing view of the children enrolled in Maharishi's flagship school, Maharishi School of the Age of Enlightenment (MSAE), located on the campus of TM's University in Fairfield, Iowa.

Viewers see several minutes of footage of uniformed boys, who appear to be about ten years old, silently filing in and out of classrooms. There are several things that seem off, not least of all that their single file lines are perfectly spaced. And something is glaringly missing: noise. Instead of the normal sounds of boisterous boys at play, who need to be told to quiet down by their teacher, these boys are mostly looking at the floor, with no interaction between each other or their teacher. There are none of the normal playful gestures one would expect to see from healthy, well-adjusted children of their age. The only sounds they make are when they are following their teacher in a song about moving waves of consciousness and the rig veda as he waves his arms up and down. The following scene is of young girls, probably around age twelve, singing in unison, in Sanskrit, from Hindu scriptures. It turns out, girls are taught separately. Not a big deal in the scheme of things, but their absence from most of the shots eerily mirrors how women show up throughout the rest of the film, in the background and underrepresented in the higher echelons of the TM organization.

In making the film, Sieveking had permission to film inside an MSAE classroom that was in session. Perhaps TM authorities woke up to the damaging effect of the classroom images and other aspects of TM that Sieveking caught on camera because, according to Sieveking, TM representatives demanded the right to edit the final cut of his documentary. Sieveking refused and says he was threatened with legal action by people representing themselves as attorneys for the David

Lynch Foundation.[6] To date, distribution of Sieveking's documentary has been blocked in the United States. It is a must view for anyone considering TM as a solution for problems in public schools. European-formatted DVDs of the film can be purchased online.

Anyone who has seen the classroom segment of the film would not be surprised to learn that enrollment at MSAE plummeted from over 700 students in early 1990s to about 220 in preschool through twelfth grade in 2012-2013. Only nineteen students graduated from the MSAE high school in 2013, and they came from nine countries.[7]

Two Unlikely Allies Fight TM

When TM leaders met during Maharishi University of Management's thirtieth anniversary in 2003, the school's president at the time, Bevan Morris, stated that traditional education left "functional holes" in students' brains; he called for consciousness-based education for "a new world of angelic individuals."[8]

Nearly forty years after the New Jersey Supreme Court's ruling, TM, primarily through the David Lynch Foundation, is still pushing TM in public schools. Apparently, they are still looking for ways around the First Amendment mandates.

In an article published on October 18, 2006, Marcus Wohlsen reported that religious clubs were allowed in California public schools under certain conditions. Quoting a spokeswoman for the California Department of Education, he wrote, "You can have a religious club as long as it is student-run and there is no church affiliation."[9]

The next day, in the October 19, 2006, issue of *Wall of Separation*, a publication of Americans United for Separation of Church and State, Rob Boston confirmed that such clubs were legal under the Federal Equal Access Act if the group was student formed and student-run.[10]

Both Wohlsen and Boston wrote their article in response to a 2006 proposal by the David Lynch Foundation to launch TM at the Terra Linda High School in San Rafael, California. The proposal, using the "club" format, called for the training of staff and students. The Lynch Foundation provided a $175,000 grant to cover the costs.[11]

Some parents weren't the only ones upset. The Pacific Justice

Institute, a nonprofit legal group that often advocates for religion to play a greater role in public life, threatened to sue the school because of TM's alleged religious nature and the faculty's involvement in the club. Two unlikely allies, Americans United for Separation of Church and State and the Pacific Justice Institute, joined forces to fight against TM in the school.

Quiet Time

"Quiet Time" is the David Lynch Foundation's term for TM in schools. It is also the title of a brochure published by the Lynch Foundation that explains how TM should work in the schools. The brochure suggests that full-time Quiet Time instructors oversee fifteen-minute TM sessions, both morning and afternoon. It further states that "extensive coaching" and "individualized follow-up support" would instill a "lifetime" practice. The material contains examples of other school activities in which TM could play a role, such as sports teams. It also describes mentoring "at-risk youth."[12]

Some parents of Terra Linda students worried that step by step, TM would infiltrate their children's lives, starting with a little "quiet time" and progressing to workshops and coaches for all aspects of life. Gina Catena, a mother of three whose children had attended Terra Linda, was outraged. She had over forty years of personal involvement in TM that included three generations of family members. Years earlier, before leaving TM, she helped introduce TM in California public schools. Based on her first-hand knowledge, Catena sent a letter to the school district and hand delivered a copy to each school board member. She also delivered a copy to the local newspaper (the same paper that had recently carried a positive story about the program).

In her letter, Catena pointed out that the "secret" mantra was an early step of thought control—keeping secrets, ostensibly for one's benefit. She spoke of authority figures that taught children to keep secrets from their parents. She also describes her firsthand experiences of how TM teachers "knowingly mislead by the omission of information."[13]

Catena then described the three follow-up meetings after initiation in which students would meditate together. Group meditation, she wrote, often created a mild trance-like or spaced-out state in which participants were more receptive to the presentation of TM dogma that follows the group meditation. Eventually, students would learn that higher consciousness was not only supremely desirable, but attainable *only* through TM and that advanced practices like the siddhis would speed the way.

The TM Club, she continued, would provide a gateway for more vulnerable teens to become absorbed. She stated that the TM organization desired those who were most inclined to take the next step, which she described as spending time at a local TM center where they would be encouraged to explore advanced meditation programs and attend in-residence programs of varying lengths. If deep rest was good, deeper rest was better, especially amongst caring and supportive meditators who imparted lifestyle guidelines to enhance their growth of consciousness. Lifestyle guidelines, she noted, would include Maharishi Ayurveda medicinal products, Gandharva Veda music, Maharishi Jyotish astrology, and Sthapatya Veda architectural plans. Of course, they would also eventually produce significant income for the TM organization.

Catena further pointed out that fully-immersed students might later seek to become TM governors, enroll in the TM nun and monk programs (Mother Divine and Purusha, respectively), attend Maharishi University of Management (MUM), and commit to a life of spreading Maharishi's unorthodox version of Hindu philosophy. When and if they had one million dollars to spend, they could aspire to the upper echelons of the movement by becoming rajas.[14]

Catena's letter had the desired effect. Upon learning that a $175,000 grant from the David Lynch Foundation for a "meditation club" would be used to teach TM to students and staff members, parents protested that TM was a form of religious practice and had no place in their public school. Reportedly, when they threatened to sue based on a violation of the separation of church and state doctrine, the Lynch Foundation withdrew the grant.

In his article for *Wall of Separation*, Rob Boston wrote, "Principal Carole Ramsey blamed the flap on 'a few parents' who created 'an environment that has led to the withdrawal for this grant.'" Boston went on to state that the "few" wanted to make certain their children would not be exposed to a religion that conflicted with their own while attending a public school. He said TM's religious elements make it illegal to teach TM in publically funded schools. He concluded by suggesting that the staff at Terra Linda read the Constitution and meditate on it, because the laudable goal of helping students relax should not depend on promoting a religion.[15] (For reference, Americans United for Separation of Church and State was involved in the New Jersey lawsuit against TM.)

The research for this book included an interview with one of the three full-time TM instructors at the Visitation Valley Middle School in San Francisco. When I told him that I was interested in learning about the school's Quiet Time program, he said that the Lynch Foundation pays all costs for TM instruction, as well as paying for daylong and weekend meditation retreats for teachers and other staff. Recently, the instructor said, some portion of the program's cost must be raised locally, as less funding had been available to support the program.

I asked if the puja ceremony had created any concern. He said that it had not been a problem because of the way the puja is presented. According to the instructor, students and teachers are told that everything comes from somewhere, and the puja is about paying respect to TM's origins. He also said that the instructors assert it's no different from karate when opponents bow to each other out of respect before a match. As far as the puja ceremony itself, he explained that they tell the students that the teacher is just singing a song. When I asked when and where students meditated, he said that the first fifteen-minute meditation period was in the class where they began their day, and the last session took place in the class where they ended their day.

As such, the TM program funded by the David Lynch Foundation does not fit the guidelines of the Federal Equal Access Act. The TM program at Visitation Valley wasn't student-run, and no one would admit that TM was a religious club. How, then, could TM be allowed in the school? I discussed the question with Rob Boston. Boston said he believed that TM flies under the radar and, as presented earlier in this chapter, the organization presents TM as a scientific technique and as a valid choice to achieve the perceived benefits of meditation.

Because it flies under the radar, TM can't acknowledge that it must withhold information about its secretive practices from parents, teachers, and school officials to gain support for its programs. This is evidenced by the minutes of an internal discussion of a proposed TM school program in Tampa, Florida or Lexington, Kentucky; the minutes aren't clear about which city is referred to. Raja Rogers Badgett, one of TM's leaders conducted the meeting. The heading for point "H" of the minutes, "Keep it private," reveals TM's overarching concern with secrecy.

> H. Keep it private.
> Jane: We are very excited about the news. Please remember to keep what we have heard private. Protect our schools. We never know what response we may get from the community. Others, who have not had the careful introduction, may not understand the program and cause trouble.
> Jeff: Even the names of the cities should not be used.
> Raja Rogers: Maharishi said there is a great power in secrecy.[13]
> Jeff: One of the principals said it leaked out that she was trying to set aside quiet time. She said she was not being secretive, but strategic. When they found out that quiet time was going to be devoted to the Transcendental Meditation technique they said, "No, no" there are other things they can do during that time. When they realized specifically that it was for the Transcendental Meditation technique she said I have to go at it differently. The principal reminded me of importance of being secretive about what steps we have made so far.
> Raja Rogers: We will get Maharishi's guidance. It may be we move very quickly and do not give the negativity time to build up.[16]

Why would any parent, teacher or school administrator want anything whatsoever to do with an organization that must sneak its way into public schools and move quickly before negativity has a chance to build up?

Lynch's National Education Summit

Leading the TM organization's effort to infiltrate public schools, Lynch has a demonstrated ability to attract "star power" to the cause, especially for fundraising. The Foundation also sponsors educational conferences in which it presents "research" targeted to the educators in attendance.

The following quote, attributed to Dr. Sidney Weinstein, former editor-in-chief of the *International Journal of Neuroscience*, appears on the research page of the David Lynch Foundation's website: "Over the past 10 years the editors and reviewers of the *International Journal of Neuroscience* have accepted several papers on Transcendental Meditation because they have met the rigorous standards of scientific publication."[17]

Dr. Weinstein retired as editor of the journal in 2008, and he passed away in 2010. Recently, Dr. Rajesh Pahwa, the current co-editor of the *International Journal of Neuroscience*, advised in an email that "Sidney Weinstein is not the Editor-in-Chief and I disagree with the statement."

On October 23, 2012, the David Lynch Foundation sponsored a National Education Summit conference held in New York City. One of the keynote speakers was Dr. John Hagelin, then president of the David Lynch Foundation and senior author of TM's much-ridiculed crime study in Washington, D.C. Here, Dr. Hagelin expanded on the flawed ADHD study presented in Chapter 6 of this book. Standing before a group of educators, he proclaimed that when ten student participants with Attention-Deficit/Hyperactivity Disorder (ADHD) practiced TM, they reversed the stress that caused ADHD and brought about marked, noticeable increases in the coherent functioning of the brain, all with just three months of twice-daily, ten-minute TM practice.[18]

The presenters used polished charts, graphs, and affirmations about TM to convince educators attending the conference that TM will work wonders in their schools. However, TM has failed to dazzle everyone. One parent posted the following on Facebook's SF Parents Against TM in Public Schools page:

> When I started asking questions about what was going on
> at my son's school in that darkened room with candles and the

windows papered over, I was told that the lawyers for SFUSD [San Francisco United School District] had never been informed about the altar, bowing, offerings, Sanskrit prayers, etc. I'm going to guess that they have since put their foot down on that. I'd be asking very pertinent questions about it if I were looking at enrolling my kid at the last schools who still allow the people in the beige uniforms to interact with our children. Are they still giving the children Hindu mantras to keep secret from everyone, including their parents? I hope not. Ask that question too. But if they aren't, why not just teach them a generic form of self-relaxation, instead of allowing our schools to be used as advertisement by the TMO, a multibillion-dollar for-profit industry, with a shady guru, and expensive levitation/flying lessons? And who in SFUSD decided that all of this is ok? I'd be asking that question, too.[19]

The mother interviewed above encouraged other parents to band together. She contends that no one should experience the personal intimidation she encountered by taking a stance against TM in her son's public school.

If Not TM, Then What?

Public schools are facing tremendous problems with few available solutions. There is no question that both teachers and students are stressed. Introducing deep rest into a school's curriculum would likely be very beneficial, but if not TM, then what?

The Relaxation Response might be well worth considering. In one promising preliminary study published in 2015, a team from the Benson-Henry Institute taught the Relaxation Response along with breathing and imagery, education on the mind/body connection, and positive psychology to teachers in a charter school. The teachers then taught the curriculum to their students. The objective was to see if a train-the-trainers model would work in a school setting; it did. Measures of stress and anxiety declined significantly, while stress management behaviors and overall classroom productivity increased.[20]

Smart Training

Until recently, the Benson-Henry Institute has limited its Stress Management and Resiliency Training (SMART) program to medical and mental health practitioners. Plans are underway to open training to more professions, including educators. Schools could designate a school nurse or teacher to earn SMART certification, and that individual, in turn, could offer Relaxation Response instruction to other teachers and students. Currently, SMART certification for the complete training program includes implementation, classroom training, and mentorship for approximately $8,500. A full description of the certification program is available online.[21]

Chapter 11

Protecting the Movement

"The only people mad at you for speaking the truth are those living a lie."

Anonymous

It Takes an Army to Defend TM's Quest for World Peace

As one might imagine, it takes a lot of focused effort to maintain TM's facade in the face of today's easy access to information. Maharishi's public persona conveyed a champion of personal and societal fulfillment, both supposedly paving the way to enlightenment. On the world stage, he wanted to be viewed as the one, supreme, personage who would usher in a new age of lasting peace and harmony. Ultimately, many came to see him as a megalomaniac with brilliant marketing skills. In *David Wants to Fly*, one long-term assistant referred to Maharishi as someone capable of using people until they ran out of money or other value to the movement and then seemingly discarding them, in his opinion, without a second thought.

TM does its utmost to stifle perceived threats. Margaret Singer, a clinical psychologist and emeritus professor of psychology at the University of California, Berkeley, was one of the leading fighters in the battle against cults. Singer pioneered research that helped define the nature and function of cults, including how they ensnare members and damage their followers and their families. During her career, as she counseled thousands of cult members and families, Dr. Singer endured numerous personal threats and attacks. In her book, *Cults in Our Midst*, she described the various forms of subtle and overt intimidation that cults use to stifle criticism and identified scholars, journalists, reporters, and writers among those who are regularly targeted.

Well-known cult harassment tactics include: enlisting or paying professionals to advocate for them, manipulating the public image, restricting and controlling research, persecuting therapists and lawyers, threatening legal suits, and forcing relatives and friends into silence. Dr. Singer also detailed an array of frightening, painful experiences—she termed them "extraordinary harassment"—that victims have endured, including herself.[1]

This book does *not* accuse the TM organization of engaging in every harassment method that Singer identified—certainly not the extreme ones. Nor does this book claim that TM is cultish in all its manifestations. However, some of the tactics that she described are recognizable in the TM organization.

The American Medical Association

The TM organization has a history of using attorneys to write threatening letters and threaten or file lawsuits to shut down criticism. During the 1990s, TM took on the American Medical Association. The scuffle began in 1991, when the editors of the prestigious *Journal of the American Medical Association* (*JAMA*) published an article, "Maharishi Ayur-Veda: Modern Insights into Ancient Medicine," written by Deepak Chopra, M.D., Hari Sharma, M.D., and Brihaspati Dev Triguna.[2] Following the requirements of most scientific journals, the first two authors submitted a signed financial disclosure form with their manuscript. With their signatures, the authors pledged they had no affiliations with TM or Maharishi Ayur-Veda (Indian herbal and medicinal products heavily marketed by the TM organization), which the article praised as preventing disease and promoting health.

Shortly after they published the article, the *JAMA* editors discovered Chopra and Sharma had vested interests in TM and its products. Embarrassed by the oversight, *JAMA* Editor Dr. George Lundberg subsequently wrote an apology to readers who were irate over the misrepresentation. "At that time," he stated, "we did not know that Maharishi Ayur-Veda, Transcendental Meditation, and the TM-Sidhi programs promoted in the article are brands of health care products and services being marketed by the TM movement."[3]

JAMA also instructed its award-winning associate editor, Andrew Skolnick, to conduct a full investigation to prevent organizations or individuals with profit motives from potentially exploiting the journal in the future. Skolnick's lengthy, investigative report of the TM organization was published in a scathing article, "Maharishi Ayur-Veda: Guru's Marketing Scheme Promises the World Eternal 'Perfect Health.'" In that piece, Skolnick stated:

> When the authors submitted their article, Chopra and Sharma were both consultants to MAPI (Maharishi Ayur-Veda Products International). During a taped telephone interview on June 17, Chopra acknowledged being a consultant to MAPI; however, in a letter faxed on June 20, he claimed he no longer had any connection to MAPI or other organizations related to the marketing company.[4]

In addition to pointing out the authors' connections to MAPI, Skolnick described a pattern of dishonest marketing practices that included attempts to link TM to scientific research. With that, he commented:

> The movement's marketing practices reveal what appears to be a widespread pattern of misinformation, deception, and manipulation of lay and scientific news media. This campaign appears to be aimed at earning at least the look of scientific respectability for the TM movement, as well as at making profits from sales of the many products and services that carry the Maharishi's name.[5]

The article hurt. In July of 1992, two TM organizations later joined by Deepak Chopra, filed a lawsuit against Andrew Skolnick, the AMA, and *JAMA's* editor-in-chief, Dr. George D. Lundberg, for $194 million.

Skolnick challenged this lawsuit as a SLAPP (an acronym for Strategic Lawsuit Against Public Participation) action—i.e., suits brought to silence critics by burdening them with legal expenses.

Skolnick wrote that the lawsuit against him failed to identify a single defamatory statement, and it was dismissed eight months later. Nevertheless, the suit was dismissed "without prejudice," meaning that TM could file again at any time it chose. In return for TM's not re-filing its lawsuit, *JAMA* agreed to consider publishing a "science article" written by TM researchers. The article TM submitted was twice rejected by *JAMA's* outside reviewers and went unpublished.[6] However, the threat of another lawsuit was enough to get the AMA to stop writing about TM. They pressured Skolnick to stop as well. Shutting the AMA and Skolnick down, and the message it sent to others, was a victory for TM.

In an October 20, 1997, cover story on Chopra, *Newsweek* magazine quoted Chopra's attorney, Michael Flynn, referenced the AMA suit as stating, "the suit was settled for an undisclosed amount." That was false. One month later, on November 17, 1997, *Newsweek* printed a correction, retracting Flynn's claim: "In our article 'DON'T MESS WITH Deepak' (LIFESTYLE, Oct. 20), we mistakenly reported that a lawsuit involving Deepak Chopra and *The Journal of the American Medical Association* was 'settled for an undisclosed amount.' In fact, there was no monetary settlement. NEWSWEEK regrets the error."[7]

The Meditation House

As reported by the *Des Moines Register* on November 30, 2011, Maharishi Foundation USA filed a trademark infringement lawsuit against The Meditation House, LLC, accusing the latter of false advertising, unfair competition, trademark infringement, trademark dilution, false representation, and unjust enrichment. Jules Green, the sole proprietor of The Meditation House, operated with no employees. The Maharishi Foundation asked the court to require Green to turn over all wrongfully generated profit from her allegedly improper activities to the foundation.

Green was indignant that the Maharishi Foundation or its licensees thought they were the only sources of knowledge of meditation and only they could teach it. She further pointed out that vedic meditation had been around for thousands of years. The *Des Moines Register* article also quoted from her website, in which she says she studied meditation in India with the "world-renowned Vedic scholar Thom Knoles." Her website further had the following disclaimer: "Jules Green and The Meditation House, LLC expressly disclaims any association with Maharishi Foundation Ltd., its programs, its methods, its trademark 'Transcendental Meditation' (the common words 'transcendental' and 'meditation' as defined in Webster's Dictionary but given an initial capital) and its licensees."[8]

TruthAboutTM.org

To combat negative research and negative press, as well as promote TM without appearing to do so, "unofficial" TM websites have been established to influence unsuspecting seekers of information. TruthAboutTM.org is one of several unofficial TM websites. It was created and is maintained by David Orme Johnson, professor emeritus at the Maharishi University of Management and author of more than one hundred TM research papers. The following description appears on the website:

> …a resource for those interested in pursuing issues and concerns about meditation effects and research, including the latest scientific research on higher states of consciousness and enlightenment. In most cases each relevant **Issue** is followed by **The Evidence**, which includes factual information (scientific research, documented facts, and events that I have personally witnessed), and **A Personal View**, which contains my own interpretations and opinions.[9]

The website exists primarily to promote positive TM research and ignore or attack negative studies. The website is not the truth about TM, in the sense that it engages in deflection and personal destruction of TM detractors.

For instance, although the Maharishi Effect has been thoroughly discredited by most non-TM scientists who have studied it, Truth-AboutTM.org identifies sixty studies that it reports have found the theory credible. However, most of the studies were self-published by the TM organization, and five were published in conference proceedings, which meant a paper was only accepted to be read at a meeting to conference attendees who chose to attend the presentation. Three papers were unpublished Ph.D. dissertations from TM institutions. On all of the nine papers published in refereed journals, David Orme Johnson and/or raja Michael Dillbeck were either the lead or included among the investigators.

TruthAboutTM.org also goes after critics on a personal level to an effort to discredit them. Dennis Roark, Anthony DeNaro, and Michael Persinger are prime examples.

Dennis Roark, Ph.D.

In July 1987, Dennis Roark, Ph.D., who served as the Maharishi International University (MIU) Dean of Faculty and chair of the Physics Department from 1975 to 1980, wrote a letter to cult expert, Pat Ryan, describing his criticisms of TM. Dr. Roark wrote, "It is my certain belief that the many scientific claims both to factual evidence of unique, beneficial effects of T.M. and physics are not only without any reasonable basis but are in fact in many ways fraudulent." As one example, he cited electroencephalogram (EEG) tests purporting to show "increased brain wave coherence while practicing the flying technique"—yogic flying. He remarked on the difficulty of taking EEG measurements of weak electric signals that would come from an array of electrodes attached to a subject's scalp while the person was hopping. Dr. Roark referenced TM's advertisements that supposedly validated the claim by depicting a "flying" meditator alongside a brainwave pattern. Roark identified the activity as energetic hopping and nothing more. The physicist also noted that the TM investigator on the study had confirmed to him that the brainwave pattern displayed on the advertisement was not of the flying/hopping meditator portrayed.

Roark also revealed that while serving as chairman of the Physics Department at MIU, the administration asked him to develop a scientific theory that would deem the flying technique a physics phenomenon. "I found then and I continue to find now such claims preposterous," Roark expressed. "This is what is normally called 'crackpot science.'" Moreover, addressing TM's assertions based upon false science and spiritual theories, he concluded that individuals who desired only an effective relaxation technique were "exposed to real dangers" and "the misleading philosophy and metaphysics claimed by its proponents."[10]

David Orme Johnson, who was the senior author of the TM study that Roark so roundly condemned, said that Roark misunderstood the methodology. Perhaps realizing the weakness of his response given Roark's stellar credentials and position within the university, Johnson then embarked on a psychological attack to explain Roark's deviance and followed that up with an attack on Roark's religion.

Johnson accused Roark of suppressing the findings of a TM study that he had conducted before joining MIU, which was that TM had no impact on one type of stress. According to Orme Johnson, Roark wanted to avoid disappointing Maharishi with negative results. Johnson claimed that Roark hadn't performed any research during his five years at MIU, asserting that the physicist had avoided research because of his guilt over suppressing the outcome of his prior study. For his final blow, Johnson portrayed Roark as a fundamentalist Christian with bigoted views about different kinds of spiritual experiences:

> ...I think that he was viewing MIU through the lens of his own conflicted feelings. He may have been 'projecting' to use the jargon of psychology. I also heard that after he started speaking out against MIU he became (or always was) a fundamentalist Christian, and I imagine that he may have had some conflicts in that area also, because the fear and antipathy towards other cultures that some fundamentalists groups instill in their followers.[11]

Anthony DeNaro

Having served as a professor of economics and business law at Maharishi International University, as well as legal counsel to MIU,

Anthony DeNaro (like Roark) was a high-level, former TM insider and an eventual target of TruthAboutTM.org and Orme Johnson.

Presenting a sworn affirmation in support of Robert Kropinski's lawsuit against TM for physical, psychological, and financial damages that Kropinski claimed were inflicted by his TM involvement, DeNaro stated, "The organization was so deeply immersed in a systematic, willful pattern of fraud including tax fraud, lobbying problems and other deceptions, that it was ethically impossible for me to become involved further as legal counsel." This affirmation contained very serious charges, which an attorney who understood the penalty of perjury would not make lightly.[12]

In retaliation, Johnson disparaged DeNaro. Instead of accusing him of being a religious zealot as he had Roark, he dismissed DeNaro as insignificant, contending no one from MIU remembered DeNaro. "I hardly knew Tony DeNaro at all," Johnson wrote, "and several other faculty that I have talked to don't even remember his ever being there."[13]

Johnson lacked any solid rebuttal so he deflected DeNaro's accusation, saying he was not equipped to talk about the research process: "That I didn't know him is significant in this context, because he, being a lawyer, was never involved in the research, so he is hardly in a position to comment on the research process. Even if he had heard second or third hand accounts, I have not heard of any specific instances cited by him to back up his claims, which are untrue."[14]

Orme Johnson's last statement is truly extraordinary. He asserts that DeNaro is lying when he claims that he doesn't even know what was said. DeNaro's 24-point indictment of TM, which reflected insider knowledge at the highest level, never mentioned research. DeNaro focused on what he considered to be the TM organization's pattern of fraud and deception. He further gave his own impression of Maharishi as having a "cavalier" attitude to reports of people being seriously damaged, and who attributed that damage to their TM practice.

Michael Persinger

In 1980, Michael Persinger, Norman J. Carrey, and Lynn A. Suess coauthored *TM and Cult Mania*.[15] Rather than responding to the substantive issues reported in the book, TruthAboutTM.org chose to attack Persinger and his colleagues:

> The book by Persinger, et al., is a diatribe against the Transcendental Meditation program and TM organization that arose from his public debates with TM teachers at Laurentian University. He sees the TM program 'as an assault on 20th-century Western civilization.' His book is an attempt to save Western civilization, which undoubtedly needs saving, but I don't think stopping the TM movement is the way to do it.[16]

SkepticsOnTM.Org

An online search to uncover concerns or complaints about TM brings up various websites, including SkepticsOnTM.org. The site's description, "What skeptics say about the Transcendental Meditation program," creates an expectation of a balanced discussion of TM. Tom Ball (a certified TM teacher in charge of the Asheville, North Carolina, TM center) created the site, which he has described as a "non-official blog that aims to provide reliable information and critical discourse for anyone interested in learning about the Transcendental Meditation program."[17]

SkepticsOnTM.org, for instance, posted the question, "Is the 'relaxation response' an alternative to Transcendental Meditation?" The answer first claims that hundreds of studies identify "the experience of transcending during TM practice," then mischaracterizes Dr. Benson's Relaxation Response as merely eyes-closed rest. Ball goes on to suggest that the relaxation technique cannot possibly deliver the range of benefits enumerated for TM. However, a recent study at the Weizmann Institute of Science in Israel attempted to understand what caused changes in brain physiology associated with mantra meditations. Important to note, the study did not use TM mantras. Instead, either the word "one" or the Hebrew equivalent—*echad*—was silently repeated at a self-paced rate. None of the subjects were experts in meditation. (Earlier we noted that Maharishi himself said that transcending was not unique to TM, that any sound could be used to transcend.)

The researchers measured brain activity using functional magnetic resonance imaging to analyze the effect of repetitive speech on the brain and compared the results to the same subjects at rest. The study reported, "Repetitive speech is sufficient to induce a largely unidirectional and widespread cortical reduced activation." In other words, just silently repeating a simple word at one's own pace appeared to cause widespread reductions in cortical activity. The reported decreases in cortical activity likely correlate with triggering the Relaxation Response, which many experience in meditation.

Apparently, silent repetition is more important than any particular sound used to meditate. It is the technique of self-paced, repetitive speech that appears to produce the results. Addressing the mantra effect, the researchers noted, "In accord with its Sanskrit translation as 'an instrument of thought,' we show that one isolated component of this practice—the element of repetitive speech even in untrained subjects—causes widespread reductions in cortical activity."[18] Meanwhile, neither the TM organization nor other independent research has presented any methodologically sound study demonstrating that TM is superior to the Relaxation Response.

Skeptics Takes on Joe Kellett

Joe Kellett, a former teacher of TM, authored an analysis of TM titled, "Falling Down the TM Rabbit Hole: How Transcendental Meditation Really Works, a Critical Opinion." Kellett acknowledged that while TM produces deep relaxation for some, who might also experience physical and psychological benefits, he also delivered a compelling argument that TM was a starting point to recruit a small percentage of TM students into something like a cult.

Ball, in response, used SkepticsOnTM.org to mount a nine-page rebuttal. In addressing Kellett's argument, Ball falsely claimed that hundreds of studies showed significant improvements in mental and physical health, with no adverse effects. He presented the following fiction as fact:

More than 600 scientific research studies have been published on the effects of the Transcendental Meditation program, involving over 20,000 subjects practicing the TM technique; no legitimate, well-controlled, peer-reviewed studies have ever found the practice to be unpleasant or harmful in any way—all such studies show positive results.[19]

Ball continued with a personal attack, alleging that Kellett had been suffering from mental illness during the time he taught TM. Specifically, Ball wrote, "One must consider the possibility that the reason the author's account of the Transcendental Meditation program differs so radically from the norm is because he is recalling experiences that were psychotic delusions."

James Krag, M.D., who is identified as a psychiatrist and a fellow of the American Psychiatric Association, actually wrote what appears to be a psychiatric assessment of Kellett that may be found on the SkepticsOnTM website. Krag theorized that Kellett became "disturbed" while practicing TM because he had a preexisting mental disorder for which the TM organization was blameless:

> [Joe Kellett] attributes the problems he developed in his life to his involvement with the Transcendental Meditation program. I think it is entirely possible that he may have developed similar problems at some point had he experienced other notable lifestyle changes. If a person develops a psychotic disorder when they enter the U.S. Army, do we say that the Army caused the problem? Do we blame the Army when the person is discharged because of it?[20]

Dr. Krag raised an issue worth noting when he stated we don't "blame" the U.S. Army. Actually, we don't blame them unless they fail to take responsibility for the soldiers under their command. The Army cares for soldiers who are wounded in action, hurt during training, or who develop post-traumatic stress disorders, even years after discharge. The Army doesn't intend for soldiers to develop mental illnesses, but takes responsibility by providing services that foster recovery, and those resources are available to those who might have been vulnerable or had a predisposition to develop such problems before enlisting. Defending TM, however, Dr. Krag further stated, "Perhaps it would be more productive for him to not criticize a specific organization that he was involved with when he became disturbed and rather to join forces with those organizations that are working to find causes and treatments for psychotic disorders."[21]

Simply put, the psychiatrist blamed the victim. Moreover, as if disparaging Kellett on one website wasn't enough, Krag's entire letter was reprinted on Orme Johnson's TruthAboutTM.org.[22] Confirming in an email to me for this book, Joe Kellett stated that he had never been Dr. Krag's patient and, in fact, had never even met him. Kellett further stated that he never consented to Krag making any comment, written or otherwise, on his mental status.

DoctorsOnTM.org

DoctorsOnTm.org, appears to be an official TM-sponsored website with a headline that reads, "Specialists answer your questions about the Transcendental Meditation program and health." The site lists about twenty illnesses with search options by topic and specialist. TM is the primary solution for every problem mentioned. An on-site search for "side effects" produced only articles about TM's effectiveness. Since there is no mention of possible TM side effects, there are no recommendations on how to deal with unwanted side effects should they occur. Notably, all the health professionals are members of The American Association of Health Professionals Practicing the Transcendental Meditation Program.

As previously noted, documents from the TM organization indicate that Maharishi was not a fan of the medical community. When asked about how TM responded to someone who complains of a serious medical or psychological problem, TM teachers have said that Maharishi would recommend that such individuals see a doctor. Many people, including friends of mine, know from painful personal or family experience that this was not the case. Maharishi told his recertified governors *not* to take help from doctors, as medical professionals give poison.[23]

Deceptive Web Page: Cheat to Compete

An online search of the terms "relaxation response" or "The Relaxation Response" produces www.RelaxationResponse.org as a top-listed option. A phone number and an email address on the site address appear to connect the website to the Benson-Henry Institute for Mind Body Medicine. One also finds a link to Dr. Benson's book, *The Relaxation Response*, on Amazon, so why not assume that the Benson-Henry Institute created the site? That would be a mistake; the site is a sham.

The content promotes Transcendental Meditation. For one thing, the presentation employs three colorful bar graphs to propose that TM is twice as effective as Dr. Benson's Relaxation Response. However, the article cited for the study that supposedly confirmed those results, "Differential Effects of Relaxation Techniques on Trait Anxiety: a Meta-analysis," never compared the Relaxation Response to TM. The diagram is a phony! A third graph references a thirty-six-year-old doctoral thesis that was published internally by TM. Of course, other clues reveal it's all a hoax. Neither the phone numbers nor the email address works.[24]

The website is so dated and poorly designed, I would have thought TM would deny any connection to it. I would have been wrong. Recently, I had an exchange with David Orme Johnson in the comments sections of the Wall Street Journal, in which I stated that research shows that the Relaxation Response is as good as TM. Remarkably, in response, Orme Johnson referenced the phony website writing:

> As for the relaxation response, there is overwhelming evidence that all meditation and relaxation techniques are *not* the same and do not have the same effects. TM is superior to other meditation and relaxation techniques on reducing trait anxiety, alcohol and drug use, and psychological health: http://www.relaxationresponse.org/ Everyone is bored with the RR and has moved on to mindfulness, which they are also becoming bored with.[25]

While I am certain Dr. Orme Johnson did not intend to say that TM was superior to other meditations in *reducing* psychological health, it appears he may also be confused about who is bored and what it is that is boring them. Given the fact that clinicaltrials.gov currently identifies 173 studies on the Relaxation Response and over 900 studies on mindfulness meditation currently underway or recently completed, compared to only fourteen for TM, the evidence is overwhelming that researchers, at least, are "bored" with TM.

I contacted the Benson-Henry Institute to see if they were aware of the website. I received the following written reply: "We are indeed aware of this site. We do not own it and have tried to have it removed."[26]

Who produced the bogus website? An investigation leads to CosmicComputer.com located in Fairfield, Iowa. The website includes a quote attributed to Maharishi: "The human brain is the hardware of the cosmic computer which, through proper programming, can compute anything."[27]

Clearly TM knows that this website is a sham. They or their surrogates created it. Incredibly, they still use it to pretend that TM is better than the Relaxation Response. Rather than referencing this website to support unproven claims of TM's superiority over the Relaxation Response, perhaps Dr. Orme Johnson could use his considerable influence in the TM organization to have the website taken down.

Online Stalkers a.k.a. Peaceful Warriors and Knowledge Kittens

People who speak out against TM online routinely see counter arguments from pro-TM bloggers. An abnormally high number of responses to anti-TM articles and the overwhelming support of positive articles leave the impression of a carefully choreographed blogging effort within the movement. Also, an unexpected volume of comments on sites with limited visibility suggest that the TM movement likely uses Google Alerts or similar services to monitor any mention of TM online and clipping services for print media.

Addressing the phenomenon, blogger Mike Doughney wondered if other anti-TM commentators felt that they were being stalked and posed the following on TM-Free Blog:

The reason I ask is that it seems that many articles that

mention Transcendental Meditation, whether they appear in an online newspaper, news service or blog, seems to attract a number of commentators - the same names and handles much of the time - who write much the same thing every time, most of it the usual TM promotional sound bites anyone familiar with TM has heard hundreds of times.[28]

Doughney was convinced that a core group of TM Bloggers was tasked with monitoring all mentions of TM online and responding in whatever way they deemed the best way to promote the organization. His suspicion was confirmed when he received the following letter from a "helpful source":

Subject: Hello Enlightened Bloggers!
To: (a redacted list of recipients)
Date: Wednesday, October 15, 2008, 5:19 PM

Dear TM Bloggers,

Hi and welcome to the world of TM blogging! I am proud to be the captain/coordinator for this group of enlightened TMers. I will be sending you web links 2-3 times a week and inviting you to visit the sites and post a response to an article, video or a reader's comment. In some cases, you will need to register with the site but it only takes 30 seconds and it will be quick next time you are directed there. The web is a powerful tool and together we can improve TM's positive presence on the web and inspire many people to take advantage of this wonderful technique. Please send me your suggestions, questions and feedback whenever you have the urge. I will help and support you in any way that I can.

PS: I am attaching the file "Tips for Bloggers" which was created by Tom Ball and has lots of great points about blogging. It will be very helpful if you save it on your computer and use it as a reference.

This link takes you to article on TM that is quite positive. However, at the end of the article, he complains about the high cost of TM and refers people to some links where they can learn meditation cheap. One link is for www.natural-stress-relief. com, which is a group of former TM teachers who teach TM via a CD for $25. This group is now under pressure from Bill Goldstein, but so far he has been unable to stop them. This group uses the TM research and says this version on the CD is the non-religious version of TM. So what you want to do is tell the author and readers of this article that you can't learn TM from CD, TM is not a religion etc.[29]

The following twelve pointers are taken from a list of thirty "blogging tips," written by Ball and which insiders were told to "keep private and not forward." A complete list, interspersed with Mike Doughney's insightful and often irreverent comments, is available online:[30]

- Rule number one: HAVE FUN DOING THIS! All your comments should be natural expressions of bliss. Then that will come across in the writing.
- Create your "blogger identity," with an ID that has a friendly, interesting, uplifting ring to it (peaceful warrior, knowledge kitten — be creative!). We recommend that you do not create multiple identities or post under different names, especially on the same site. Sometimes the owner of the site can see the IP addresses and will know. Honesty is our policy.
- As a general rule, best if posts are short, not over 100 words. Otherwise, people may tend to avoid reading them...
- On sites such as YouTube, Google, and many other formats you can create a profile that is visible to the public. It is a good idea to fill out the profile and create an identity that will convey your credentials, achieve-

ments, interests, etc., so that people who look will find you credible.

- Write as a TM teacher speaking to the public: cool head, warm heart, to the point—always dignified and uplifting.
- It's OK to be personal; in fact, it's most convincing. You don't want to sound like an official of some organization. And it can be good to refer to your own personal experience of TM's benefits, those of your family, friends, etc. It may sometimes be useful to say how many years you've been meditating.
- When responding to confused or negative comments, it is crucial that we NEVER criticize or condemn the author of those remarks, and never say directly that the PERSON is wrong. There's no need to draw attention to the person at all. In such cases, we address only the false claims that are being made, and simply state the facts, referring to scientific research when relevant...
- It is fair to state directly that a particular claim is untrue or a misunderstanding, but refrain from using inflammatory adjectives such as, 'preposterous,' 'absurd,' insane,' 'bogus,' 'whacko,' etc...
- If you are ever stumped about how to respond to a particular negative claim, contact your team captain and if necessary we will research the question.
- It's best not to copy and paste ALL of your responses, however, because if someone exposes that you are doing this it could discredit you. Generally, blogs are meant to be personal statements
- Definition of 'Rajas': The meaning of the word 'raja,' in the context in which it is used in the TM organization, is 'administrator.' Just as many professions have their uniforms, such as the military, the rajas have theirs: as professional peacemakers.
- **Whatever negative claim is asserted, however well**

they might argue it, remember that it is always simply flat-out wrong — their most ardent and rational-sounding arguments always contain the seeds of their own undoing. You know from your own experience that TM is 100% natural, innocent, and good, and you can always refer to your self-referral experience — saying that you have experienced the benefits directly, and over 300 peer-reviewed scientific research studies support TM's benefits. (Bold added.)

Enlightened Bloggers in Action

On June 6, 2016, Joy Victory, deputy managing editor of Health-NewsReview.org, posted "Conflicts of interest abound in NYT post on Transcendental Meditation" in which she criticized the *New York Times* for printing an article touting TM in the schools as a news feature rather than an opinion piece.[31] According to Victory, that it was an opinion piece was revealed only in the last line of the article, which identified the writer as Norman Rosenthal. Rosenthal is a psychiatrist and TM advocate who has authored popular books on TM and is a frequent expert speaker at TM fundraising events.[32]

Within forty-eight hours, Victory's article had fourteen comments. In such a short timeframe, what was the likelihood that fourteen people with detailed knowledge about TM would learn of the piece published in an online health newsletter and be so highly motivated to post comments? How many were TM bloggers?

Tomas Ball, the author of the TM blogging points, posted two of the responses. His first lengthy post addressed TM's trademarking and deflected Victory's primary critique by comparing TM and the Relaxation Response. The Relaxation Response was not mentioned in Victory's article. His second post highlighted the tactics of TM's apparent blogger in chief:

Tomas Ball
June 7, 2016, at 6:56 am
Generally, respectably-sourced news pieces on TM in recent

years have been highly positive, based on facts and actual reports from schools where the TM/Quiet Time program is having such a beautiful, life-changing impact.

Considering TM's well-established track record, it's rare when a writer with an axe [sic] to grind decides, for whatever reason, to take such an intensely negative angle. I find such cynical perspectives to be based on misunderstandings, misconstrued facts and misinformation, as with this article.

The most glaring false assertion here is that the TM organization produced a "profit of $65 million" according to 2014 tax records; the facts are indeed public record, and that is not what they say, and there is no evidence to back up for the writer's claim. The reality is that there is no profit—and basically, there never has been. The TM organization in the US operates at breakeven, and all the funds generated by course fees go back into the organization to make TM available to more people, especially at-risk populations who cannot afford to pay a course fee. Most of the 500,000-plus people who've learned TM in the past 10 years have learned for free. Part of every course fee funds someone to learn who can't afford to pay. No one in the TM organization has ever financially profited from TM, from the bottom to the top. TM is truly non-profit. Check the IRS records.

The claim that the scientific research has not been "scrutinized" is also false. TM has probably been subjected to more independent critical review boards, scientific review boards, and peer-reviewed research than any other self-development program. See http://www.truthabouttm.org. The review presented above to refute claims of TM's benefits carries little weight by itself, when you consider the selection critic used in that limited study, but I wonder if the author of this article considered such factors. As other commentators here have shown, many other larger, independent reviews have confirmed TM's unique range of effects, including a major study (2013) by the American Heart Association, which determined that TM is the only form of meditation effective against hypertension (the report stated that mindfulness "cannot be recommended" to lower high blood pressure).

It is also blatantly false to state that most of the research studies "have deep ties with TM employees." Look at the bibliography of over 750 studies, you probably won't find any that were done entire [sic] by meditating scientists and the TM organization has never funded a research study. Most of the recent funding has come from the NIH. Those few studies that did include scientists associated with Maharishi University of Management were almost always led by non-TM-related scientists from other universities, who requested that these scientists be on the team.

It is also false that Dr. Norman Rosenthal, the former 20-year senior NIH researcher and professor of psychiatry at Georgetown University, has any ties to the TM organization.

And finally, it's not "Transcendental Meditation followers" bringing TM to schools, it's the schools themselves. In almost every major city there is a waiting list of schools who have approached the David Lynch Foundation and TM program, as in the small city where I live. I have never known "TM people," as one calls them, to proselytize TM in the schools. School principles [sic] learn about the independent scientific research on TM, and they reach out, because they know they need these results, which no other meditation program has yet been shown to produce.

PS, wild claims of levitation? Completely irrelevant—and who is claiming anyone can levitate? Not me.[33]

My Response to Ball the Blogger

Ball did not identify his affiliation with the TM organization. Aside from his role as a chief TM blogger and the creator/administrator of SkepticsOnTM.Org, he is a longtime TM teacher and TM center director. In a departure from his own blogging guidelines, Ball delivered a personal attack on the writer. He then claimed TM was a non-profit, break-even operation in the U.S. If that's true in any sense, TM's ability to raise money has put most for-profit organizations to shame.

A lengthy investigative article by *India Today* in June of 2012, valued Maharishi's wealth in India at his death at 60,000 Indian crores, or approximately US$9.33 billion. Most of the value was in land, comprising 12,000 acres across India, including many prime locations. That estimate was exclusive of other real estate holdings throughout the world, as well as various businesses, schools, universities, television stations, etc.[34]

The *Economist* estimated the value of TM's real estate holdings in 1998 at over US$3 billion (just under US$5 billion in current value [2017]). That figure did not include the many businesses, schools, and universities in TM's portfolio.[35]

In the documentary *David Wants to Fly*, another raja mentioned recently raising over $200 million to construct a new Brahmasthan in India. The total budget for the project: $400 million. Maharishi lived in a 200-room palace in Holland. Planes, helicopters, and fleets of cars were owned by the organization; all were at his disposal.[36]

Ball mentioned that most of the 500,000 people who have learned TM over past decade have learned for free. Perhaps he would be willing to provide documentation to support this claim and define "free." Perhaps Mr. Ball could also weigh in on just how Maharishi accumulated billions of dollars in assets if so many people were learning for free.

Next, Ball misrepresented the American Heart Association study he references by stating that the AHA determined that TM was the only form of meditation effective against hypertension. The AHA said that TM might have a modest effect on hypertension, and they didn't know if TM was better in this regard than any other meditation: "It is not certain whether it [TM] is truly superior to other meditation techniques in terms of BP lowering because there are few head-to-head studies. As a result of the paucity of data, we are unable to recommend a specific method of practice when TM is used for the treatment of high BP."[37]

In fact, an official of the AHA said that TM had embarrassed the organization by exaggerating study findings on TM and hypertension for its commercial purposes.[38]

Ball also claimed that few studies involved scientists from MUM, and even those featuring MUM scientists included lead scientists from other universities. Even a cursory view of TM studies shows that most have TM-affiliated researchers as the lead investigator or as part of the research team. In fact, eleven of the fourteen current TM studies shown on ClinicalTrials.gov are MUM-based, and all fourteen identify a MUM scientist as the principal investigator.[39]

Ball additionally claimed that Dr. Norman Rosenthal didn't have any ties to the TM organization. Dr. Rosenthal is an expert presenter at TM conferences, including the David Lynch Foundation. In fact, Rosenthal recently received an award for "Lifetime in Service to the Public's Health" from the Foundation. He offers testimonials on the TMHome.com website, as well as writes newspaper articles supporting TM research. He also authored two books on the benefits of TM. TM advocates like Dr. Rosenthal prompted Joy Victory to condemn the *New York Times* for treating what she considered an opinion piece as news.

Ball also claimed a demand existed for TM in schools, giving the impression that TM adherents have not been active in promoting the adoption of TM in public schools. The fact is that the David Lynch Foundation, supporting its stated goal of teaching TM to public school students, has sponsored conferences for educators and held major fundraisers to pay for Quiet Time programs in schools. Funds are also used to pay an estimated sixty staff members employed by the Foundation in its offices located in New York, Washington, D.C., Los Angeles, and Chicago.

To discount TM's association with levitation, Ball added a postscript, calling it a "wild claim." From the mid-1970s until his death in 2008, Maharishi himself made wild claims about levitation. TM-Sidhi courses that teach levitation (yogic flying) continue to be offered several times a year by the TM organization. In fact, one recent five-day TM course in Brussels featured a Yogic Flying competition as well as "rounding"—TM's euphemism for more frequent and longer meditation periods.

Unkosher Meditation

An unsolicited response to an article on TM provides another il-
lustration of TM's blogging points in action. In May 2016, Rabbi Tzvi
Freeman wrote an article, "Kosher Meditation," for a Jewish online
publication, Chabad.org. The mantras used in TM, he wrote, were
names of Hindu deities; consequently, the TM meditation practice
would not be appropriate for a Jew.[40]

Rabbi Freeman subsequently received an email that challenged his
statement. Knowing that I had been a TM teacher, Rabbi Freeman gave
me a copy of the email and asked my advice regarding how to reply.
He said he often received similar correspondence from TM advocates.
The lengthy justification as to why the mantras had nothing to do
with Hinduism and, therefore, did not conflict with Jewish theology
or practice, came from Evan Finkelstein:

> I was on the TM Teacher Training course for about 6 months,
> at the end of which time I received the mantras from Maha-
> rishi that I was to give to others when teaching them the TM
> technique. They [sic] were a good number of them and none of
> them were the names of Hindu gods. I know this because I was
> interested in the study of comparative religions and knew well
> the names of the many so-called 'Hindu personal gods.' I say
> 'so-called Hindu personal gods' because according to Maharishi
> Mahesh Yogi the Sanskrit term Devata, which is usually trans-
> lated in English to mean G-d or gods, is very badly translated
> and misinterpreted.... For Maharishi, to gain the support of the
> Devata is to gain the support of G-d's laws or forces of nature
> that G-d generated according to G-d's will... The names of the
> various Devata are the names of the fundamental qualities and
> powers of that One infinite Being. Because of my experiences
> with TM over many years and because of a thorough study of
> all of Maharishi's teachings over those years, and as a Jew who
> studied Torah and Talmud at Yeshiva University and continues
> to love and practice my Jewish Tradition, I can say without any
> doubt in my heart that I am a better Jew.

Although Finkelstein portrayed himself as a run-of-the-mill TM teacher with an interest in comparative religions, he neglected to mention that he held a Ph.D. in Maharishi Vedic Studies from Maharishi International University, where he spent his entire academic career, until his recent retirement, as a professor of vedic studies and comparative religion.[41]

On December 22, 2004, Maharishi held a press conference during which he stated, "In the transcendental field, there is the Constitution of the Universe where all the Devatas, all the fields of creative intelligence—vishnu, shiva, [Hindu gods] all vedic devatas—[reside]. They're all there…" Maharishi openly says that devatas in vedic literature are the names of Hindu gods. Given his academic credentials and teaching background, it is profoundly disingenuous for Finkelstein to feign ignorance of something so fundamental to his field of study.[42]

Chapter 12

TM Casualties

According to proponents, TM never or only rarely leads to an undesirable outcome. Should any negative consequence surface, true believers contend that an individual's preexisting condition has caused the problem; moreover, the impact would have been worse without TM. In reality, negative consequences happen often enough for TM to have a phrase, "something good is happening," which sometimes means the meditator is in danger.

Since TM is marketed as a technique to lower stress and improve health (a promise of enlightenment comes later), the meditation practice appeals to individuals who might have underlying issues to address. In fact, a belief that TM may help with these very issues may motivate some people to start. TM teachers, however, do not screen candidates for possible psychiatric issues, nor does the TM organization provide any meaningful assistance should a problem emerge.

The public deserves a straightforward answer to the question of whether meditation—TM or otherwise—is safe for all. Research *not* sponsored by the TM organization and affidavits from people formerly holding high positions in the TM organization have associated TM with a broad range of negative reactions. Negative results are much more prevalent among those who meditate more frequently and for longer periods each time. While they might experience more profound problems with greater frequency, difficulties, although rare, can at times occur with beginners who adhere to the recommended twenty minutes or so in the morning and evening each day.

Medical practitioners spend years to acquire the education and experience to treat patients. TM teachers, who, in most instances, have no medical or mental health training, oversee (albeit in a limited context) the well-being of all kinds of students. Thus, the TM teacher may fail to recognize potentially severe reactions to TM instruction. In fact, there is no mention of possible adverse effects in the introductory lectures preceding TM instruction, and they aren't mentioned after instruction unless someone has a problem. TM teachers created "checking notes" instructing them how to handle pain and discomfort that might arise even within the first days of TM instruction, demonstrating that the organization is well aware of these problems.[1]

When I became a TM teacher, we were told to minimize discussions about anything negative the new meditator might have experienced, such as sensations, movements, and pressure anywhere in the body, including the heart or head. We were instructed to tell the student that "something good is happening" and to continue meditating, even if the sensation felt strong and showed no sign of diminishing or dissolving. Furthermore, even with substantial pain, the student is told to endure it with anticipation that the discomfort, at whatever level, might continue in almost every meditation until the "wound" resolves. The teacher often says that what, at times, manifests as severe discomfort is due to an actual physical "wound" of stress somewhere in the body that meditation is, no doubt, resolving. Not one iota of empirical evidence validates that explanation.[2]

The Checking System

When I taught TM, teachers followed a systematic procedure to check and guide each student through the correct process of meditation. It entailed a series of brief exercises (for instance, sitting quietly with eyes closed for thirty seconds), then meditating for three minutes. After each exercise, we'd ask questions and proceed based on whether the student answered *yes* or *no* regarding the exercise just completed.

For example, if sitting quietly was easy for the student, then a three-minute meditation would be the next exercise. If not, the teacher used a different procedure. Major sections of the process were designed to deal with the meditator's reporting any of a wide variety of experiences that could be deemed distressing.

Overall, checking was a way to debug a person's meditation. Checking followed a rigid format, which resembled a flowchart: if this, then that. We were instructed not to deviate from the checking procedure.

At times, an individual's stress was transient, so demonstrating patience and friendly concern usually allowed the student to adjust easily. In other instances, a degree of undue effort or strain would creep in, but once the individual let go, all would be right again. Some, however, experienced difficulties that interfered with normal daily functioning or created ongoing symptoms of a troubling severity. In those situations, TM's one-size-fits-all formula presented real problems. If a person was having problems, the proper intervention was to use the checking notes to enable them to have a correct experience of meditation. Period.

Some people have pre-existing, sometimes quite serious, psychological problems. Arguably, a disproportionate number of such individuals are attracted to TM or other remedies they think might help. Unless things have dramatically changed, TM teachers are not trained to recognize such situations and provide proper referrals.

Shaking and body movements, as well as overpowering thoughts, while rare, are common enough even during the first few meditations that an entire section of TM's checking procedure is devoted to these severe symptoms. Students are told to view potentially frightening experiences as a release of stress, and new meditators are advised not to resist the symptoms because they are beneficial. If the shaking becomes violent and seemingly out of control, then students are told to open their eyes and wait until it subsides and eventually stops.[3]

As if uncontrollable shaking and overpowering thoughts aren't bad enough, in the case of "severe problems" that might arise, the checking notes allow the ill-equipped, untrained TM teacher to inquire if the student has seen a doctor. Because the TM teacher has no access to a student's health information unless the person volunteers it, and there is no indication to new students that this information could be useful to prevent potentially dangerous side effects, no one can make an informed decision as to whether someone would be better off not learning TM.[4]

The frequency of severe problems is unknown, not only because TM doesn't provide information about the adverse effects. Instead, they deny they exist. One nineteen-year-old student described his first TM experience in the comments section of an article about TM and hypertension on CardioBrief.org. He complained that he received no information about possible side effects until after he had paid for the course. His account delivers a wake-up call:

> The very first session, I had pains/pressures in the right side of my head and a weird sensation throughout the right side of my body. By the 4th day of the workshop, I ran out into the hall at the beginning of the group meditation session because my eyes had clenched shut, and I couldn't open them for a bit. I lay out in the hall on the ground with sharp pains in my head like a knife being dragged down the side of my face. My entire body was shaking, my muscles tense, and I sobbed and cried uncontrollably. I was instructed to meditate only for 5 minutes instead of the full 19 minutes. The shorter meditation sessions, however, did not help as it got to the point where all this stuff would start happening shortly after closing my eyes to meditate. I stopped meditating after a particular session where I experienced very painful facial contortions for 3 hours after the meditation session was over. Unfortunately, stopping meditation did not stop these symptoms because they surfaced whenever I was relaxed (not trying to meditate), whenever I'd get stressed, and they even happened at random. My symptoms became full-blown in July at summer camp after giving meditation another shot, and I had what superficially looked like convulsions and could not walk without assistance afterwards because my abdominals were clenched so tight, I was hunched over more than 90 degrees (that occurred on and off for nearly a

week before having another attack, that time more severe). The doctor at camp informed me it was conversion disorder (neuropsychiatric illness in which stress/emotions are not properly processed causing physically unexplainable involuntary motor/sensory symptoms), gave me Ativan (which actually helped, the symptoms vanished for a number of hours but came right back after it lost its effect), and told me to see a psychiatrist when I got home. I told my meditation teacher about it, and at first, he believed it was a spiritual experience, a kundalini experience, but after e-mailing him a video of part of an attack, he was shocked as he'd never seen such a violent reaction to meditation and told me to go see a doctor.

I've had a variety of symptoms since then that have affected me for much of the day most days including speech problems, dystonia (limbs locking up, facial contortions, full body contortions), pains all over my body, extreme mood swings, gait problems, convulsions, episodes of hysterical screaming and flailing/thrashing (which can last up to 3 hours), uncontrollable hysterical laughing and other verbal outbursts, abnormal body movements, tics, tremors, insomnia, de-realization, panic attacks, chronic anxiety, paralysis, and the list goes on. I had never before in my life had motor problems before taking the TM course. I wasn't involved with the organization long enough or knew enough about it to have anything against them, but I am against dishonesty. I'm rather perturbed because of the organization's false advertising, claiming that there are NO negative side effects, and yet they discuss the negative side effects AKA de-stressing after you pay for the course. And anything negative is portrayed as something positive and desirable (which I guess if that's how you choose to view it, then there are no 'negative' effects) and thus encouraged. There is nothing glamorous about being plagued daily by debilitating neuropsychiatric symptoms at 19 years old. 'De-stressing' shouldn't cause you more stress than is being 'released' and more stress than you have experienced in your lifetime.[5]

A retired professor stated in an affidavit that he had attended a two and one-half month TM teacher-training course with Maharishi in India in 1969. While on the course, he experienced his body twisting and turning involuntarily. He further felt pressures and sensations inside his skull, and sometimes had difficulty controlling the forces, movements, and sensations. Others on the course had similar experiences and formed a group to meet with Maharishi to see if he could help their situations. Despite several meetings, Maharishi offered no antidote for them. The professor's problems that initially emerged in India became more intense and uncontrollable, occurring several times during the day, and he stopped teaching TM in 1975. Not any of the medical doctors he consulted over the years were able to help, and he blamed TM for all his physical disorders.[6]

Former Maharishi International University professor and legal counsel, Anthony DeNaro, described what he characterized as abnormal TM-related behaviors while working at the University. In his sworn affirmation (dated July 16, 1986) DeNaro wrote that many of his students were spaced-out, unfocused, zombie-like automatons who were incapable of critical thinking. The consequences of regular and intensive meditations were so damaging and disruptive to the nervous system that students could not complete assignments. Many could not enroll in or continue with their academic programs. The excuses they gave for not being able to sit for an examination or write a paper included having a "bad meditation" or just "got off rounding" (group TM) and hadn't gotten "back to earth yet."

DeNaro had previously been a professor of law and economics at Hofstra University, Adelphi University Graduate School, and Cornell University School of Labor and Industrial Relations when he was hired in November 1975, by Maharishi International University as legal counsel. Also, he had a full-time teaching schedule in economics and business law. He stated in his affirmation that he was privy to internal "secret" (but not privileged) correspondence as well as conversations with the principal leaders of the TM movement and University, including Maharishi himself. In that capacity, he said that he witnessed a system of denial and avoidance, as well as outright lies and deception, to cover up or sanitize serious problems on campus. These included nervous breakdowns, episodes of dangerous and bizarre behavior, threats of and actual attempted suicide and homicidal ideation, psychotic episodes, crime, depression, and manic behavior that accompanied rounding (intensive group meditations).[7]

March 1, 2004, is almost eighteen years after DeNaro wrote his affirmation. How much did MUM change during that period? Not much, it would appear. March 1, 2004, is the date MUM student, Shuvender Sem, fatally stabbed another MUM student in the University cafeteria. Earlier that day, Sem stabbed another student in the face with a pen during a class ironically called "Teaching the Age of Enlightenment." That student required seven stitches at a local hospital to close the wound. He was lucky.[8]

After consulting a psychologist, MUM administrators decided Sem would have to leave the university on a flight the next morning. According to one newspaper report, Sem was taken to the on-campus apartment of the dean of students where he was supposed to be under supervision. Left unattended, Sem took a paring knife from the dean's kitchen and went to the dining hall. The dean reportedly followed Sem to the dining hall, watched while he interacted with other students, but did not take him back into custody. Ten minutes later, without provocation, Sem stabbed another student, a freshman, four times in the chest, killing him.[9]

The police weren't called after the first stabbing earlier that day. Critics charged a cover up to prevent negative publicity, which MUM denied. Lawsuits were filed against the University and the Maharishi Vedic Development Education Corporation charging gross negligence for ignoring warnings that Sem was dangerous, for failing to report the first attack to police as required by the university's own policies, for failing to provide medical attention to the injured student, and for failing to control the scene properly, causing delays in the emergency response. The suits further alleged that staff members said the attacks occurred because Sem was not meditating properly, and that the twice-daily practice of Transcendental Meditation, which the university requires of all students, can be dangerous for people with psychiatric problems. The lawsuit against MVED was dismissed; the lawsuit against the University was settled out of court in 2009.[10]

Maharishi's response to the murder of an nineteen-year-old freshman at his university was that MUM bore no responsibility for the tragedy. As reported in the Guardian, Maharishi blamed the murder of on US foreign policy, "Dr. Craig Pearson, executive vice-president of Maharishi University, said: 'Maharishi Mahesh Yogi has made one comment regarding this event. He said that this is an aspect of the violence we see throughout society, including the violence that our country [the United States] is perpetrating in other countries.'"[11]

In the 1990s, anti-TM websites appeared as TM teachers and meditators grew disillusioned with Maharishi. Web hosts and others who made accusations often chose to remain anonymous. They may have feared retaliation by the organization and shunning by fellow meditators, including friends and family members who might still have been caught up in the movement.

TranceNet.net, a repository for TM information, was created in 1995 and last updated in 2007. It contained first-person accounts of individuals claiming to have been damaged by TM. Many posts give only the writer's first name. Many were likely painful to write, but apparently, people felt compelled to expose the damage they attributed to their TM experiences. There are thirty-one personal stories on the site; a few are presented in this chapter with permission of the writers.[12] One man, for example, told about his TM teacher-training course:

> I was involved for seven years. It all ultimately came to a head in 1976. The movement went into a new phase, and Maharishi started talking about siddhis, powers, and techniques for doing levitation and other things. This created so much cognitive dissonance in me that I didn't know what to do. I had to find out if it was real or not, and I wanted to believe that it was real, but something in me said that it couldn't possibly be real. People weren't really going to levitate. So I went to Switzerland for the sixth-month course on 'powers.' I went,

and I fell apart. They were using us as experimental subjects. There was fasting involved and various austerities that come out of Hindu traditions, enemas and various bizarre food combining rituals. A lot of madness got released. After five months of this I said whatever problems I might or might not have, TM is not making them better, it is making them worse and I decided to leave. This was like leaving everything, because I had severed all of my other ties and relations: no job, no career, no marriage and no prospects. I got up in the middle of the night and walked to the train station. I felt like I was crossing from slavery into freedom, from one intolerable situation into the great unknown. By the way, no one really levitates. I fully satisfied myself as to that.[13]

Others have suffered emotionally from compromising their religious convictions. A Jewish woman, for instance, was dating a TM teacher—he had a Ph.D. from MIU—who purchased TM instruction as a birthday gift to her. Although Jewish, he didn't know much about Judaism, but seemingly had "an infinite knowledge of Hinduism, although he didn't call it that." The woman trusted her boyfriend; besides, she was interested in other cultures. He'd told her that TM was not a religion, and even though learning TM required that her teacher perform a ceremony, she would only watch.

Her initiation took place in her TM teacher's home. She knew that he and his family strongly identified as Jewish, and the ambiance of their home reflected that. Thus, when he took her into a little incense-filled room with an altar, she was caught off guard. "I was profoundly uncomfortable with this 'whole other world' I had entered," she expressed:

Still, I remained and tried to appear 'calm.' As I watched this young Jewish man bow down to this graven image, I was sick. I felt my heart beating faster, and I could barely repeat my mantra when that part of the ceremony began. It's difficult for me to describe what I was thinking or feeling, in fact, my memory is unclear. I believe I was desperate to escape into the mantra and meditation to rid my mind of what I thought to be a hideous act of betrayal....

Later, the woman was relieved to locate TM-EX and TranceNet, two anti-TM websites. She wrote,

> I will never be able to adequately express my gratitude. There was not one problem I had with TM/MMY that wasn't echoed over and over again. Whatever I had imagined was worse, much worse. The impact of the 16 mantras being the names of Hindu gods caused me to feel profound guilt and shame. What flashed before my eyes was my family members, dead and living, all part of the proud Jewish continuum. I thought about how my Yiddish-speaking grandmother might feel about me invoking the energy of a Hindu god. I will never erase the image of... bowing down to the picture of MMY's dead teacher. Once I saw a translation of the puja, I was 'stunned,' not however too shocked to read on. The information was overwhelming.[14]

The German Study

The German Government's Ministry of Youth, Family, and Health commissioned a research project to study TM in Germany that was completed in 1980. The study, "An Empirical Analysis of Pathogenic Structures as an aid in Counseling," was prompted, in part, by the growth of TM's popularity in the 1970s and the many severe problems attributed to TM that were reported to German authorities by parents, spouses, and ex-meditators. To date, it's the most thorough study of TM regarding the comprehensive study protocols used and the preparation of interviewers who conducted the study.

The TM organization challenged the release of the study but failed. On May 24, 1982, in Case number 7 C 2.87, Germany's highest federal administrative tribunal, the Bundesverwaltungsgericht, ruled:

1. The Federal Government is competent and allowed to care about cults.

2. The Federal Government is allowed to warn of TM.
3. The Federal Government is allowed to designate TM a "Youth Religion" as well as a "Psych group."
4. The Federal Government is allowed to say that TM is taught by teachers who are not qualified [to deal with TM caused problems].
5. The Federal Government is allowed to say TM can cause psychic defects or destruction of personality.[15]

One section of the study described how TM deceived the public by claiming it was a scientific technique, while the teaching and practice of TM could be understood only in the context of Hinduism. The authors referred to Maharishi, who demanded obedience from teachers and officers, as having "become increasingly more, what he in fact always was; an exceptionally old-fashioned Hindu, who therefore does expect a retreat from the activities of living."

The study participants were parents or spouses whose loved ones had developed severe problems they attributed to TM. Also included were those who had stopped TM because of problems they attributed to its practice. Most of the study participants meditated significantly longer than twenty minutes twice a day; however, many reported that they were encouraged to extend the length of their meditations by TM teachers, at TM centers, or while attending weekend or longer TM courses. The study serves as a cautionary tale, because TM's recertified governors devote six hours a day to their TM practice, and advanced courses continue to feature more frequent meditation periods.

Of sixty-seven participants interviewed, thirty had one or more children practicing TM who exhibited strong social or mental transformations. Ten married couples participated; however, only the non-meditating partner was interviewed. Twenty-seven ex-meditators who had practiced TM for an extended period and were directly affected by TM also took part. Parents and spouses interviewed were considered indirectly affected. Many interviewees were afraid of retaliation or reprisals. Thus, all participants received anonymity. A team of three people conducted each interview. The team included one teacher, a doctor of education or a person skilled in working with socially handicapped, and a note taker. The interviews were recorded and lasted between two and three hours.

The results affirmed one of the major suppositions of this book: TM has two faces, one public and one hidden. The public face includes regular meditators who do not attend advanced TM courses. In general, they have little to do with the TM movement. Investigators found that 88.5 percent of individuals in this group meditated for the official time of two twenty-minute sessions; four percent meditated up to two hours; another four percent meditated up to four hours daily.[16]

On the hidden side were people who attended courses that featured longer meditation periods. Half increased their meditation time from forty minutes to a period ranging from two to four hours per day. Course leaders were reported as having encouraged longer meditation times and urged course attendees to get more involved in movement activities.

Spending on TM courses varied between regular meditators and TM insiders (siddhas, teachers, governors). Regular meditators spent between $4,000 and $8,000 on TM. Insiders, on average, spent $70,000 on courses. More extreme devotees spent $200,000 to $300,000 for advanced courses (the approximate U.S. dollar value in 2017).[17]

The findings revealed that many meditators experienced severe mental disturbances, including disturbed sleep, anguish, problems with concentration, hallucinations, and feelings of isolation, depression, and over-sensitivity. More than 70 percent of the meditators said mental disturbances had originated from meditation. Whether they were ordinary meditators who had little contact with TM or more committed, many of their complaints were similar. As the investigators reported, meditators were left helpless:

> The unconscious sense impressions and visions which are brought to the conscious mind during meditation cannot be controlled by the meditator himself. The mainly positive experiences in the earlier stages (pictures, feelings of happiness) are replaced in time - according to reports of the ex-meditators - by

terrifying images and feelings of fear or anguish. This is known to the T.M. movement.[18]

Follow-up procedures for TM students experiencing serious problems were almost nonexistent. Regardless of the experience, "just keep meditating" and "something good is happening" were TM teachers' most common responses—instructions that often added to already dangerous situations that many study participants could not resolve without outside help.[19]

The study also identified a detrimental effect on decision making, with some losing self-determination and turning to TM teachers for guidance on important life decisions. The study further showed that many participants experienced changes in facial expression, posture, voice, and handwriting, often indicating severe personality alterations. Of such individuals, 75 percent identified these traits as negative, and 12 percent thought they were positive.

Physical problems also resulted. Before practicing TM, the study's participants reported average health, but 63 percent noted physical complaints while meditating. The most common were stomach and bowel issues, headaches, insomnia, and neck pain—all of which were known to the TM organization.

In 76 percent of the cases, psychological disorders and illnesses occurred. Nine percent of meditators had undergone treatment before TM, but when practicing, the proportion increased to 43 percent who had psychiatric treatment or required medical treatment. The most prevalent psychological disorders were tiredness (63 percent), states of anxiety (52 percent), depression (45 percent), nervousness (39 percent), and regression (39 percent). The study showed that 26 percent had a nervous breakdown, and 20 percent expressed serious suicidal tendencies. Pre-existing psychological illnesses got worse after beginning TM.

The comprehensive research by the German government documented just how devastating TM can be on practitioners, their families, and their spouses.[20]

Sometimes a Hero

Combating Cult Mind Control, a book by Steven Hassan, has a chapter on courageous survivors. One of the stories is about Gina Catena, whom I have come to know in researching this book. Gina is much more than a survivor; I consider her a hero.

Gina was a child of the TM movement. Her parents learned TM in the 1960s. Her father believed that TM would cure his crippling arthritis. In 1974, Gina, then a young teenager, was sent to live and go to school at MIU. Like many TM children, she remembers raising herself while her parents meditated for hours on end or traveled to expensive, advanced TM training courses.

Both in Fairfield (TM's mecca) and in the global TM community, she witnessed people experiencing troubling symptoms, including severe physical and mental problems. She learned of suicides that families hushed up, family and loved ones who were self-medicating with expensive Maharishi-branded herbal concoctions, and spending thousands of dollars on Hindu prayer ceremonies to treat a variety of illnesses. People often did not get medical or psychological care because they were told Maharishi frowned on Western medical practices. Gina believes that refusing treatment might have contributed to the death of some. Some went bankrupt spending money on any TM products they thought would speed enlightenment.

By 1988, with three children, Gina had had enough of TM life. She convinced her second husband to move to California. They were later divorced. She started taking classes at a community college and, while raising her children, earned three degrees. Today she works as a certified nurse midwife and nurse practitioner in a large medical center in Northern California. She also serves as a voluntary member of the Advisory Board of the International Cultic Studies Association. She focuses on children raised in cults.

Gina writes and speaks as a volunteer about the risks of TM that she believes contributed to financial losses, psychological instability, and medical devastation for many of her loved ones. She further participated in the successful fight to contest the David Lynch Foundation's introduction of a large TM program at the Terra Linda High School in

San Rafael, California. She remains concerned that secrecy surrounds TM instruction, which lacks informed consent of the risks inherent in the program, and that it serves as an entree to an alternate society that might create severe problems for vulnerable people.[21]

In 2014, Gina agreed to make a presentation at the Commonwealth Club in San Francisco. She shared stories of close friends who ended up with severe physical and psychological problems; some committed suicide. She said she believed their TM practice caused or exacerbated their problems. She talked about her father, who died a slow, painful death from crippling arthritis. He refused medical treatment, relying on unproven Maharishi herbal products, Hindu prayer services, and gemstones, costing many thousands of dollars. Gemstones and various certificates he had received for his dedication to Maharishi surrounded his deathbed. A once-accomplished professional, Gina's father succumbed to promises of healed karma, aligned chakras, and spiritual reconciliation. He died having spent his entire estate plus $80,000 in credit card charges—his final donation to Maharishi and a debt that family was left to resolve. Her informative and moving talk is available online.[22]

During a question-and-answer session following Gina's presentation, one person took the microphone and introduced himself as a founder of the Berkeley TM center and Maharishi International University. He also claimed that he taught TM to one thousand people. Later, he said, he ran highly successful businesses. Responding to Gina's presentation, he contended that while TM had its share of nutty people in the movement, nutty people were everywhere. He also "strongly" suggested that Gina had presented "only her personal version" of TM, which did not in any meaningful way represent TM or the TM movement.

In an email to me, Gina told me that time constraints prevented her from responding to the man's remarks. Had time allowed, she wrote, she would have made the following comment:

[His] admission that there are nutty people in the TM Movement is typical of the rationale used by TM's true believers; nutty people are everywhere, as are unstable people, as are suicidal people. She would have asked him, how does he or any TM true believer, reconcile the promise of Maharishi that TM will solve problems, anxiety, poverty, and instability? If TM successfully fulfilled its promises, then such problems should occur with significantly less frequency, or not at all, especially among long term TM devotees in TM's Fairfield community.

The fact is that a group of young adults raised in TM joined with others to address such concerns because they tired of having so many loved ones commit suicide or turn to substance addictions. They formed an interdisciplinary coalition called 'Fairfield Cares.' If TM did as promised, there would be no need for such an organization.[23]

Here was a woman who, from childhood, experienced tragedies amongst her family and friends, and through sheer willpower managed to forge a successful life. Her questioner said, "It was only her personal version." After fifty years of practicing TM, his stance is without caring or understanding. After all, for protectors of the movement, Gina's experience and those of so many others does "not in any meaningful way represent TM or the TM movement."

Parting Thoughts

There are several alternative forms of meditation/relaxation that work at least as well as TM without many of the harmful potential side effects or exposure to an organization that seems to put money and expansion before people.

The TM organization is penetrating the public-school system under the guise of science. But they do not simply want to instruct children in a stress-relieving technique. What is really happening is that non-accredited, non-vetted adults are taking children out of class to participate in a Hindu prayer service, and then encouraging them to recite the names of Hindu gods twice a day, everyday. But they don't stop there. They want to get involved in our children's lives, to coach them, and lead them in school clubs, to slowly expose them to an alternative lifestyle that is secretive and manipulative, all with the intention of familiarizing them with Maharishi's concept of enlightenment and world peace. The ultimate goal, of course, is having children become life-long, financially contributing members of the TM world.

TM instruction in public schools should be a particularly disturbing thought to parents across the country. It is also illegal. The people running the TM charade have been successful at covering this fact up. They rely on inundating people with "scientific" studies, celebrity, and TM hype.

As we've seen, people who criticize TM may be opening themselves up to personal attack by TM surrogate websites, such as TruthAboutTM.org and SkepticsonTM.org. And the TM organization has threatened legal action when they've felt threatened or violated. It is understandable that most people would not want to take on the tremendous burden of a court case. Even assuming attorney fees and court costs are covered, there is an enormous amount of time involved in litigation. This should not be an issue for school boards who have not only the responsibility of protecting our children, but also of following the law. Going to court is a last option, not the first. School boards could simply close down any TM programs in their districts without involving the courts.

If this book only serves as a compilation of interesting information about Maharishi and the organization he created, writing it will have been a waste of time. From my perspective, the value of this book will be gauged by how many people currently doing TM stop, and how many considering TM don't start because of what they've learned in these pages — and that parents and educators use this information to get TM out of our public schools.

Resources

The links below are from the TM-Free Blog (http://tmfree.blogspot.com) which describes itself as providing insider information about Transcendental Meditation techniques, the TM movement and Maharishi Mahesh Yogi. It also provides independent, skeptical and critical views of TM claims and research, and also reports allegations of deception by TM organizations. The links below reference important resources, many of which are used in this book.

Please carefully note the Disclaimer/Intellectual Property notice below that also appears on the TM-Free blog website.

Essential Documents:

TM and TM-Sidhi Techniques: http://minet.org/mantras.html
TM Mantra Meanings: http://minet.org/www.trancenet.net/secrets/mantras.shtml
TM Initiation and Checking: http://minet.org/www.trancenet.net/secrets/checking/index.shtml
TM Children's Initiation: http://minet.org/www.trancenet.net/secrets/checking/child.shtml

TM "Holy Tradition" – Initiation Ceremony: http://minet.org/www.
trancenet.net/secrets/puja/tradt.shtml

TM Initiation Ceremony – True Meaning: http://minet.org/www.
trancenet.net/secrets/puja/alternate.shtml

TM-Sidhi "yogic flying" program: http://minet.org/www.trancenet.
net/secrets/sutras/

Wikileaks "Transcendental Meditation" category: https://wikileaks.
org/wiki/Category:Transcendental_Meditation

Roark Letter: http://www.minet.org/Documents/roark-letter

DeNaro Affidavit: http://minet.org/www.trancenet.net/law/denarot.
shtml

Kropinski's Answer to Interrogatory No. 40: http://minet.org/www.
trancenet.net/personal/40.html

Kropinski trial testimony "Soma and the Gods": http://minet.org/
www.trancenet.net/secrets/soma/index.shtml

Malnak v. Yogi decision 1977: http://minet.org/www.trancenet.net/
law/nj/nj1.html

JAMA – Maharishi Ayur-Veda (Andrew Skolnick): http://www.
aaskolnick.com/mav.htm

How to Design a Positive Study: Meditation for Childhood ADHD:
https://spacecityskeptics.wordpress.com/2009/01/07/how-to-
design-a-positive-study-meditation-for-childhood-adhd/

Abstracts of Independent Research on Transcendental Meditation:
http://minet.org/www.trancenet.net/research/abs.shtml

Problems with TM Research – Barry Markovsky: http://minet.org/
www.trancenet.net/research/markovsky.shtml

Evaluating Heterodox Theories, including "Maharishi Effect"
(Markovsky and Fales): http://minet.org/www.trancenet.net/
research/markovsky2.shtml#theory

Maharishi's Proposal for Permanent World Peace (2001 newspaper
ad): http://media.doughney.net/2011/maharishi-proposal-
ad-20010923.pdf

TM Critic/Skeptic Links:

Minet.org (including TM-EX Archives): http://minet.org
"Falling Down the TM Rabbit Hole" by Joe Kellett: http://www.
    suggestibility.org
Behind the TM Facade: http://www.behind-the-tm-facade.org
Mumosa.com: http://mumosa.com
Rick Ross' TM Page: https://www.culteducation.com/group/1195-
    transcendental-meditation-movement.html

Cult Recovery Links:

CounterCultSearch.com (search for counselors, info, more): http://
    countercultsearch.com
reFOCUS – Recovering Former Cultists' Support Network: http://
    www.refocus.org
Freedom of Mind Resource Center: https://freedomofmind.com
Intervention 101: http://intervention101.com/
Wellspring Retreat & In-Residence Recovery Center: http://
    wellspringretreat.org
Colleen Russell, MFT, Bend, Oregon: http://www.colleenrussellmft.
    com
Bill & Lorna Goldberg, New Jersey: http://www.blgoldberg.com

Cult Research Links:

International Cultic Studies Association (ICSA): http://www.
    icsahome.com
Cult NEWS 101: http://cultnews101.com/
ex-cult Resource Center: http://www.ex-cult.org
Edmonton Society Against Mind Abuse: http://www.esama.ca

Disclaimer/Intellectual Property Notice

All posts are the personal opinions of the individual authors and are not necessarily endorsed by other TM-Free contributors, individually or collectively. Comments on articles are the sole responsibility of the authors themselves. All postings are copyrighted by the individual authors and all rights are reserved by them.

The TM-Free Blog and its contributors do not offer instruction in, or assistance with, meditation or any other mental practice. The blog's title should not be interpreted to mean that this blog offers a "free" meditation practice of any kind.

Transcendental Meditation, TM, TM-Sidhi and many other terms used on this website are trademarks of Maharishi Vedic Education Development Corporation (MVED) and/or Maharishi Foundation USA, as explained at great length. All material on this site is intended for information, commentary, criticism, parody, satire, and other journalistic purposes. Any use of copyrighted, service marked, or trademarked material is therefore subject to fair-use exception under US Copyright Law.

TM-Free Blog is a critical resource on Transcendental Meditation; by this we mean that our web site focuses on material that is critical of the TM program. We offer our site not as a complete answer to questions about TM, but rather as a balance to the largely unbalanced and uncritical resources published by the numerous TM movement organizations and their participants. TM-Free contributors do not conclude that any group discussed on this site is necessarily cultic or abusive in nature. We provide suppressed and alternative information so that you may make informed decisions — for yourself.

Notes

Waking Up: Why I Wrote This Book and Why Now?

1. Chaim Miller, *Turning Judaism Outward* (Brooklyn NY: Kol Menachem Press, 2014), 347-353

Chapter 1: My Story

1. Allan I. Abrams and Larry M. Siegel, "The Transcendental Meditation Program and Rehabilitation At Folsom State Prison: A Cross-Validation Study," *Criminal Justice and Behavior*, 1978; 5(1): 3-20. https://doi.org/10.1177/009385487800500101
2. siddhi. Dictionary.com. *Dictionary.com Unabridged*. Random House, Inc. http://www.dictionary.com/browse/siddhi (accessed September 27, 2017)

Chapter 2: Behind the Veil

1. "Beacon Light of the Himalayas, 3 of 4: Theory of Spiritual Development," TranceNet, last modified March 28, 1997; hereafter cited as "Beacon Light Theory." http://minet.org/www.trancenet.net/secrets/beacon/beacon2.shtml
2. Hindu.com Website http://www.hinduwebsite.com/symbolisminpuja.asp

3. The Quiet Time Program Brochure https://www. davidlynchfoundation.org/pdf/Quiet-Time-Brochure.pdf
4. "Maharishi Mahesh Yogi," Obituary, *Economist*, February 14, 2008. http://www.economist.com/node/10683705
5. Transcendental Meditation Domain of Atlanta Directors Meeting Notes, 2005-2007 https://wikileaks.org/wiki/ Transcendental_Meditation_Domain_of_Atlanta_ Directors_ Meeting_Notes,_2005-2007
6. The Holy Tradition http://minet.org/www.trancenet.net/secrets/ puja/tradt.shtml
7. Malnak v. Yogi, 440 F. Supp. 1284 (D.N.J. 1977). http://law.justia.com/cases/federal/district-courts/ FSupp/440/1284/1817490/
8. Ibid.
9. "Beacon Light Theory."
10. "Beacon Light Theory."
11. "Beacon Light of the Himalayas, 2 of 4: Maharishi's Discourse," TranceNet, last modified March 28, 1997. http://minet.org/ www.trancenet.net/secrets/beacon/beacon1.shtml
12. "The TM and TM-Sidhi Techniques," Meditation Information Network, accessed September 27, 2017. http://minet.org/ mantras.html
13. "What's Your Mantra Mean?" TranceNet, last modified September 26, 1997. http://minet.org/www.trancenet.net/ secrets/mantras.shtml
14. Paul Mason, *Roots of TM*, (U.K: Premanand, 2015), 274-275.
15. "What is the Transcendental Meditation Mantra?" YouTube video, 1:41. Posted by "Transcendental Meditation," February 22, 2010. https://youtu.be/_0rbfSaRwCU

Chapter 3: What's in a Name?

1. "Beacon Light of the Himalayas, Notes," TranceNet, last modified March 30. 1997. http://minet.org/www.trancenet.net/ secrets/beacon/notes.shtml

2. *David Wants to Fly*, directed by David Sieveking (2010; Berlin: Neue Visionen).

3. "Sexy Sadie Lyrics: Beatles," Metrolyrics, accessed September 27, 2017. http://www.metrolyrics.com/sexy-sadie-lyrics-beatles.htm

4. "The Maharishi Song: John Lennon," Genius, accessed September 27, 2017. https://genius.com/John-lennon-the-maharishi-song-lyrics

5. Judith Bourque, *Robes of Silk Feet of Clay: The True Story of a Love Affair with Maharishi Mahesh Yogi, the TM guru followed by the Beatles, Deepak Chopra, David Lynch, and millions more.* (Estonia: Printing Partners Group, 2015).

6. David Mertens, "Sexy romps of the Beatle's giggling guru," Cult Education Institute, August 23, 1981. https://www.culteducation.com/group/1195-transcendental-meditation-movement/20543-sexy-romps-of-the-beatles-giggling-guru.html

Chapter 4: Religious Roots & Money Motives

1. *Fort Lauderdale News*, August 6, 1977, 5.

2. *Palm Beach Post*, June 24, 1977, 70.

3. Herbert Benson MD, *Beyond The Relaxation Response: The Stress-Reduction Program That Has Helped Millions of Americans* (New York: Berkley, 1985), 156-158.

4. "TM-Sidhi Technique – Sutras," Other Documents, Meditation Information Network, accessed September 29, 2017. http://minet.org/Documents/FREE-Sidhis

5. "One Million Dollar Paranormal Challenge," Wikipedia, last modified August 22, 2017. https://en.wikipedia.org/wiki/One_Million_Dollar_Paranormal_Challenge

6. "Governor Recertification Course: Overview of Policies & Procedures," Wikileaks, accessed September 27, 2017. https://file.wikileaks.org/file/tm-governor-course-2005.pdf

7. "Resolution of the Governors of the Age of Enlightenment on the Auspicious Day of *Rām Navami* of the Vedic Calendar," Wikileaks, accessed September 27, 2017. https://file.wikileaks.

org/file/transcendental-meditation-governors-resolution-apri l-18-2005.pdf

8. "Maharishi Exposed," YouTube video, 13:46. Posted by "juz111," December 4, 2010. https://youtu.be/rGc1yTDU8Fs

9. "Governor Recertification," section 5.

10. Mario Orsatti, "Health tips from Dr. Oz," TM Blog, April 8, 2010. http://www.tm.org/blog/people/dr-oz-reveals-his-daily-transcendental-meditation-practice/

11. "Governor Recertification," section 6.

12. "Governor Recertification," section 7.

13. "Governor Recertification."

14. Associated Press, "Reclusive Guru's in battle to Demolish Historic Dutch Monastery," Cult Education Institute, January 20, 1998. https://www.culteducation.com/group/1195-transcendental-meditation-movement/20480-reclusive-gurus-in-battle-to-demolish-historic-dutch-monastery.html

15. "Your Donation Can Sponsor a Maharishi Yagya," Maharishi Yagya Program, accessed September 28, 2017. https://www.maharishiyagyaprogram.eu/donate.html

16. "Maharishi Special Yagyas," Maharishi Vedic Pandits, accessed September 28, 2017. http://vedicpandits.org/yagya/special-yagya/

17. *David Wants to Fly*, directed by David Sieveking (2010; Berlin: Neue Visionen).

18. Ibid.

19. "Vedic Pandits go 'missing' in US, reports Hi India," *India Today*, January 26, 2014; hereafter cited as India Today. http://indiatoday.intoday.in/story/vedic-pandits-go-missing-in-us/1/339928.html

20. "Only 5% pandits missing: Maharishi vedic university," *Times of India*, January 28, 2014. http://timesofindia.indiatimes.com/world/us/Only-5-pandits-missing-Maharishi-vedic-university/articleshow/29488769.cms

21. "Vedic Pandits go 'missing' in US, reports Hi India," *India Today*, January 26, 2014; hereafter cited as India Today. http://

indiatoday.intoday.in/story/vedic-pandits-go-missing-in-us/1/339928.html

22. "Law enforcement respond to Vedic City unrest," YouTube video, 3:49. Posted by "KTVOtv," March 11, 2014. https://www.youtube.com/watch?v=XnDgm1gXaAg

23. "Missing Pandit Brutally Killed," CultNews101, September 5, 2014. http://www.cultnews101.com/2014/09/missing-pandit-brutally-killed.html

24. John Greenfield, "How a tiny town in Iowa became 'Silicorn Valley'," Chicago Reader, May 31, 2017. https://m.chicagoreader.com/chicago/fairfield-iowa-transcendental-meditation-silicorn-valley-mantra/Content?oid=26743992

25. Home Page, Maharishi Jyotish Program, accessed September 27, 2017. http://www.maharishijyotishprogram.eu

26. Home Page, The Mother Divine Program, accessed September 27, 2017. http://www.motherdivine.org

27. "Mother Divine, TM's Celibate Nuns," TranceNet, last modified July 27, 1997. http://minet.org/www.trancenet.net/secrets/thmd.shtml

28. "Taste of Blissful Life Course," The Mother Divine Program, accessed September 27, 2017. www.motherdivine.org/courses/a-taste-of-blissful-life/iowa/

29. Home Page, Maharishi Purusha Program, accessed September 27, 2017. www.purusha.org

30. Ibid.

Chapter 5: TM's Real Golden Boy

1. http://www.mum.edu/assets/achievements/images/roth_doctorate.pdf

2. Personal communication

3. *David Wants to Fly*, directed by David Sieveking (2010; Berlin: Neue Visionen).

4. "What is the Transcendental Meditation Mantra?" YouTube video, 1:41. Posted by "Transcendental Meditation," February

22, 2010. https://youtu.be/_0rbfSaRwCU

5. Robert Roth, *TM-Transcendental Meditation* (Iowa: Maharishi University of Management Press, 2011) Appendix B.

6. https://www.amazon.com/gp/product/B004OA6LWS/ref=oh_ aui_d_detailpage_o00_?ie=UTF8&psc=1

7. Robert Roth, *TM-Transcendental Meditation* (Iowa: Maharishi University of Management Press, Ibid.

8. https://www.amazon.com/gp/product/B074ZLL1Y7/ref=oh_ aui_d_detailpage_o01_?ie=UTF8&psc=1

9. https://en.wikipedia.org/wiki/Transcendence_(philosophy)

10. "Beacon Light of the Himalayas, 3 of 4: Theory of Spiritual Development," TranceNet, last modified March 28, 1997.

11. https://www.nytimes.com/2017/10/20/health/social-media-fake-news.html

12. Alexandra Wolfe, "Transcendental Meditation for Everyone," Wall Street Journal, June 30, 2017.https://www.wsj.com/articles/ transcendental-meditation-for-everyone-1498842465#livefyre-toggle-SB10232408185146533862504583235663476792892

13. https://wikileaks.org/wiki/Transcendental_Meditation_Domain_ of_ Atlanta_Directors_Meeting_Notes,_2005-2007

Chapter 6: Is TM a Cult?

1. Michael D. Langone, "Characteristics Associated with Cultic Groups" *ICSA Today*, 2015; 6(3): 10. http://www.icsahome.com/ articles/characteristics

2. Steven Hassan, *Combating Cult Mind Control: The #1 Best-selling Guide to Protection, Rescue, and Recovery from Destructive Cults* (Newton, MA: Freedom of Mind Press, 2016), 92-95.

3. "TM Initiator's Oath," TranceNet, last modified February 24, 1997. http://minet.org/www.trancenet.net/secrets/puja/oath. shtml

4. Michael D. Langone, ed., *Recovery from Cults: Help for Victims of Psychological and Spiritual Abuse* (New York: W.W. Norton, 1995), 129-139.

5. Anonymous, email message to author, July, 15, 2017.

Chapter 7: Faulty Research

1. "transcendental meditation," Results Page, ClinicalTrials.gov, accessed September 28, 2017. https://www.clinicaltrials.gov/ct2/results/displayOpt?flds=a&flds=b&flds=c&submit_fld_opt=on&term=transcendental+meditation&show_flds=Y
2. "mindfulness," Results Page, ClinicalTrials.gov, accessed September 28, 2017. https://www.clinicaltrials.gov/ct2/results?cond=&term=mindfulness+&cntry1=&state1=&Search=Search
3. "mbsr," Results Page, ClinicalTrials.gov, accessed September 28, 2017. https://www.clinicaltrials.gov/ct2/results?term=mbsr&Search=Search
4. "relaxation response," Results Page, CliinicalTrials.gov, accessed September 28, 2017. https://www.clinicaltrials.gov/ct2/results?term=relaxation+response&Search=Search
5. MB Ospina et al., "Meditation Practices for Health: State of the Research." *Evidence Report/Technology Assessment* 2007 JUN; 155: 1-263. https://www.ncbi.nlm.nih.gov/pubmed/17764203
6. Madhav Goyal MD et al., "Meditation Programs for Psychological Stress and Well-being: A systematic Review and Meta-analysis," *JAMA Internal Medicine* 2014; 174(3): 357-368. https://doi.org/10.1001/jamainternmed.2013.13018
7. J.S. Hagelin et al., "Effects of Group Practice of the Transcendental Meditation Program on Preventing Violent Crime in Washington, DC: Results of the National Demonstration Project, June-July 1993," *Social Indicators Research* 47(2), 153-201. https://doi.org/10.1023/A:1006978911496
8. Robert Park, *Voodoo Science: The Road from Foolishness to Fraud* (Oxford: Oxford University Press, 2000), 28-31.
9. Hagelin, "Effects of Group Practice," http://istpp.org/crime_prevention/
10. Park, *Voodoo Science.*

Aryeh Siegel

11. Peter Woit, *Not Even Wrong: The Failure of String Theory and the Search for Unity in Physical Law* (New York: Basic Books, 2006), 205-206.

12. Andrew A. Skolnick, "The Maharishi Caper: Or How to Hoodwink Top Medical Journals," *Science Writers*, Fall 1991. http://www.aaskolnick.com/naswmav.htm

13. I received this information in a conversation with a source who requested anonymity. May 23, 2017

14. "Pagels Letter," TranceNet, last modified October 9, 1997. http://minet.org/www.trancenet.net/research/pagels.shtml

15. "Fairfield, IA: Crime Rates," Neighborhood Scout, accessed September 28, 2017. https://www.neighborhoodscout.com/ia/fairfield/crime

16. Donna Cleveland, "Suicide in Fairfield: Iowa town struggles with mental health awareness," Little Village, September 26, 2014. http://littlevillagemag.com/suicide-in-fairfield-iowa-town-struggles-with-mental-health-awareness/

17. "TM and healthy, normal blood pressure," Transcendental Meditation News & More, March 4, 2015. https://tmhome.com/benefits/transcendental-meditation-and-blood-pressure/

18. "What are the evidence-based benefits? A Healthier Heart," accessed October 1, 2017. www.TM.org

19. Robert D. Brook et al., "Beyond Medications and Diet: Alternative Approaches to Lowering Blood Pressure," *Hypertension* 61 (May 2013): 1360-1383. https://doi.org/10.1161/HYP.0b013e318293645f

20. Ibid.

21. Stephen Propatier, "American Heart Association promotes alternative therapy for hypertension." Skeptoid, posted on May 1, 2013. https://skeptoid.com/blog/2013/05/01/american-heart-association-promotes-alternative-therapy-for-hypertension/

22. "Dr. Steinbaum endorses meditation," Transcendental Meditation News & More, July 17, 2014. http://tmhome.com/books-videos/heart-disease-treatment-tm-meditation/

23. Louise Hartley et al., "Transcendental meditation for the primary

208

prevention of cardiovascular disease," *Cochrane Database of Systematic Reviews* 12 (2014): CD010359. https://www.ncbi.nlm.nih.gov/pubmed/25436436

24. Robert H. Schneider, "Evidence for Upgrading the Ratings for Transcendental Meditation: Response to AHA Scientific Statement on Alternative Methods and BP (Letter to the Editor)," *Hypertension* 62 (November 2013): e42. http://hyper.ahajournals.org/content/62/6/e42?ijkey=eddde0ae80469d55d080e160bd73a32cdd248779&keytype2=tf_ipsecsha

25. Robert D. Brook and Joel W. Hughes, "Response to Evidence for Upgrading the Ratings for Transcendental Meditation: Response to AHA Scientific Statement on Alternative Methods and BP (Letter to the Editor)," *Hypertension* 62 (November 13, 2013): e43. http://hyper.ahajournals.org/content/62/6/e43.full

26. Robert H. Schneider et al., "Stress Reduction in the Secondary Prevention of Cardiovascular Disease: Randomized, Controlled Trial of Transcendental Meditation and Health Education in Blacks," *Circulation: Cardiovascular Quality and Outcomes* 2012; 5: 750-758. https://doi.org/10.1161/circoutcomes.112.967406

27. Larry Husten, "Archives Decides At Last Minute Not to Publish a Scheduled Paper," Cardio Brief, June 27, 2011. http://www.cardiobrief.org/2011/06/27/archives-decides-at-last-minute-not-to-publish-a-scheduled-paper/

28. Larry Husten, "New Concerns Raised About Withdrawn Archives Meditation Paper," Cardio Brief, June 28, 2011. http://cardiobrief.org/2011/06/28/new-concerns-raised-about-withdrawn-archives-meditation-paper/

29. Larry Husten, "Investigator Defends Controversial Transcendental Meditation Paper," Cardio Brief, November 20, 2012. http://cardiobrief.org/2012/11/20/investigator-defends-controversial-transcendental-meditation-paper

30. Larry Husten, "Yet Another Look At The Transcendental Meditation Paper," Cardio Brief, November 25, 2012. http://cardiobrief.org/2012/11/25/yet-another-look-at-the-transcendental-meditation-paper

31. Husten, "Another Look."
32. "Dr. Robert Schneider explains the new approach to tackling heart disease," Transcendental Meditation News & More, posted on June 14, 2017. https://tmhome.com/benefits/dr-robert-schneider-md-heart-health-transcendental-meditation/
33. Husten, "New Concerns Raised."
34. Ibid.
35. Husten, "Yet Another Look."
36. Vernon A. Barnes, PhD, John L. Rigg, MD, and Jennifer J. Williams, LCSW, VA, Rigg JL, Williams JJ. "Clinical Case Series: Treatment of PTSD With Transcendental Meditation in Active Duty Military Personnel," *Military Medicine* 2013; 178(7): e836-40. https://doi.org/10.7205/milmed-d-12-00426
37. Brian Rees et al., "Significant Reductions in Posttraumatic Stress symptoms in Congolese Refugees Within 10 days of Transcendental Meditation Practice," *Journal of Traumatic Stress* 2014; 27(1):112-115. https://doi.org/10.1002/jts.21883
38. Ibid.
39. Joshua Z. Rosenthal, MD, et al., "Effects of Transcendental Meditation in Veterans of Operation Enduring Freedom and Operation Iraqi Freedom With Posttraumatic Stress Disorder: A Pilot Study," *Military Medicine* 2011; 176(6): 626-630. http://militarymedicine.amsus.org/doi/pdf/10.7205/MILMED-D-10-00254
40. "A RCT of Meditation Compared to Exposure Therapy and Education Control on PTSD in Veterans," ClinicalTrials.gov, last modified August 5, 2016. https://www.clinicaltrials.gov/ct2/show/NCT01865123?term=transcendental+meditation&rank=7
41. "Veterans statistics: PTSD, Depression, TBI, Suicide," Veterans and PTSD, last modified September 20, 2015. http://veteransandptsd.com/PTSD-statistics.html
42. "How to Design a Positive Study: Meditation for Childhood ADHD..." Space City Skeptics, posted January 7, 2009. https://spacecityskeptics.wordpress.com/2009/01/07/how-to-design-a-positive-study-meditation-for-childhood-adhd/

43. Ibid.

44. Ibid.

45. David W. Orme-Johnson and Michael C. Dillbeck, "Methodological Concerns for Meta-Analysis of Meditation: Comment on Sedlmeier et al. (2012)," *Psychological Bulletin* 2014; 140(2): 610-6. https://www.ncbi.nlm.nih.gov/pubmed/24564175

46. Charles Elder et al., "Effect of Transcendental Meditation on Employee Stress, Depression, and Burnout: A Randomized Controlled Study," *Permanente Journal* 2014 Winter; 18(1): 19-23. https://www.ncbi.nlm.nih.gov/pmc/articles/PMC3951026/

47. http://www.tm.org.nz/less-anxiety

48. https://consensus.nih.gov/1995/1995behaviorrelaxpaininsomnia ta017html.htm

49. James S. Brooks and Thomas Scarano, "Transcendental Meditation in the Treatment of Post-Vietnam Adjustment," *Journal of Counseling and Development* November 1985; 64:212-215. https://doi.org/10.1002/j.1556-6676.1985.tb01078.x

50. Charles Elder et al., "Reduced Psychological Distress in Racial and Ethnic Minority Students Practicing the Transcendental Meditation Program," *Journal of Instructional Psychology* 2011; 38(2): 109-116.

51. Elder, "Effects of Transcendental Meditation," 19-23.

52. P.C. Ferguson et al., "Psychological Findings on Transcendental Meditation," *Journal of Humanistic Psychology* 1976; 16: 483-488.

Chapter 8: The Relaxation Response

1. Robert K. Wallace, Herbert Benson, and Archie F. Wilson, "A wakeful hypometabolic physiologic state," *American Journal of Physiology* 1971; 221(3): 795-799.

2. Herbert Benson, *The Relaxation Response* (New York: HarperTorch, 2000), 32-33.

3. "Guided Meditations and DVDs," Benson-Henry Institute,

accessed September 29, 2017. https://www.bensonhenryinstitute.
org/meditation-cd-and-dvd/

4. Benson, *The Relaxation Response.*
5. Benson, *The Relaxation Response*, 30-31.
6. Herbert Benson, *Beyond The Relaxation Response: The Stress-Reduction Program That Has Helped Millions of Americans* (New York: Berkley, 1985), 3-8.
7. Herbert Benson, *Relaxation Revolution: The Science and Genetics of Mind Body Healing* (New York: Scribner, 2010), 109-112.
8. "Published Research," Benson-Henry Institute, accessed September 29, 2017. https://www.bensonhenryinstitute.org/research-published-research/
9. James E. Stahl et al., "Correction: Relaxation Response and Resiliency Training and Its Effect on Healthcare Resource Utilization." PLoS ONE 2017; 12(2): e0172874. https://doi.org/10.1371/journal.pone.0172874
10. "SMART Certification," Benson-Henry Institute, accessed September 29, 2017. https://www.bensonhenryinstitute.org/training-apply-for-certification/

Chapter 9: Is Meditation for Everyone?

1. "The TM and TM-Sidhi Techniques," Meditation Information Network, accessed September 27, 2017. http://minet.org/mantras.html
2. Mindful Magazine, https://www.mindful.org/jon-kabat-zinn-defining-mindfulness/
3. Mind the Hype: A Critical Evaluation and Prescriptive Agenda for Research on Mindfulness and Meditation Nicholas T. Van Dam, Marieke K.van Vugt, David R. Vago, LauraSchmalzl, Clifford D. Saron, AndrewOlendzki, Ted Meissner, Sara W.Lazar, Catherine E. Kerr, JolieGorchov, Kieran C. R. Fox, Brent A.Field, Willoughby B. Britton, Julie A.Brefczynski-Lewis, David E. Meyer *Perspectives on Psychological Science* First published date: October-10-2017

4. Daniel Goleman, and Richard Davidson, *Altered Traits: Science Reveals How Meditation Changes your Mind, Brain and Body* (New York, NY: Penguin Random house LLC, 2017) 2017

5. Ibid., 207

6. Lindahl JR, Fisher NE, Cooper DJ, Rosen RK, Britton WB (2017) The varieties of contemplative experience: A mixed-methods study of meditation-related challenges in Western Buddhists. PLoS ONE12(5): e0176239. https://doi.org/10.1371/journal.pone.0176239

Chapter 10: TM in Public Schools

1. "Maharishi Message from Beyond the Grave?" TM-Free Blog, posted by "Laurie" on November 6, 2014. http://tmfree.blogspot.com/2014/11/maharishi-message-from-beyond-grave.html

2. David J. Bardin, "Meditation, Delusion and Deception," ICSA, accessed September 29, 2017. http://www.icsahome.com/articles/meditation--delusion-and-deception-bardin

3. Malnak v. Yogi, 440 F. Supp. 1284 (D.N.J. 1977). http://law.justia.com/cases/federal/district-courts/FSupp/440/1284/1817490/

4. "Malnak v. Yogi, 592 F. 2d 197 – Court of Appeals, 3rd Circuit 1979," Intervention101, posted on February 13, 2014. http://www.intervention101.com/2014/02/malnak-v-yogi-592-f-2d-197-court-of.html

5. TM-Free Blog, January 19, 2001 http://tmfree.blogspot.com/2011_01_16_archive.html

6. *David Wants to Fly*, directed by David Sieveking (2010; Berlin: Neue Visionen).

7. Joseph Weber, *Transcendental Meditation in America: How a New Age Movement Remade a Small Town in Iowa* (Iowa: University of Iowa Press, 2014), 120.

8. "M.U.M. celebrates 30th anniversary, advocates meditation in education," Cult Education Institute, posted on September

16, 2003. https://www.culteducation.com/group/1195-transcendental-meditation-movement/20630-mum-celebrates-30th-anniversary-advocates-meditation-in-education.html

9. "California school loses funds over meditation controversy," Cult Education Institute, posted on October 18, 2006. https://www.culteducation.com/group/1195-transcendental-meditation-movement/20523-california-school-loses-funds-over-meditation-controversy.html

10. "Transcending The Constitution?: Calif. School Drops Plans To Promote Hindu Meditation Program," Americans United, posted on October 19, 2006. https://www.au.org/blogs/wall-of-separation/transcending-the-constitution-calif-school-drops-plans-to-promote-hindu

11. "California school loses funds over meditation controversy," Cult Education Institute, posted on October 18, 2006. https://www.culteducation.com/group/1195-transcendental-meditation-movement/20523-california-school-loses-funds-over-meditation-controversy.html

12. "The Quiet Time Program" Brochure, David Lynch Foundation, accessed September 29, 2017. https://www.davidlynchfoundation.org/pdf/Quiet-Time-Brochure.pdf

13. "Letter to San Rafael School Board..or.. How TM Lures the Young and Vulnerable," TM-Free Blog, posted on January 13, 2007. http://tmfree.blogspot.com/2007/01/letter-to-san-rafael-school-boardor-how.html

14. Ibid.

15. "Transcending The Constitution?: Calif. School Drops Plans To Promote Hindu Meditation Program," Americans United, posted on October 19, 2006. https://www.au.org/blogs/wall-of-separation/transcending-the-constitution-calif-school- drops-plans-to-promote-hindu

16. https://wikileaks.org/wiki/Trancendental_Meditation_Domain_of_Atlanta_Directors_Meeting_Notes,_2005-2007

17. Research Page, David Lynch Foundation, accessed September 29, 2017. https://www.davidlynchfoundation.org/research.html

18. "How to Design a Positive Study: Meditation for Childhood ADHD…" Space City Skeptics, posted January 7, 2009. https://spacecityskeptics.wordpress.com/2009/01/07/how-to-design-a-positive-study-meditation-for-childhood-adhd/

19. SF Parents Against TM in Public Schools, Facebook, posted June 24, 2016. https://www.facebook.com/SF-Parents-Against-TM-in-Public-Schools-201123776750702/

20. HK Wilson et al., "Teacher-led Relaxation Response Curriculum in an Urban High School: Impact on Student Behavioral Health and Classroom Environment'" *Advances in Mind-Body Medicine* 2015; 29(2): 6-14. https://www.ncbi.nlm.nih.gov/pubmed/25831429

21. "SMART Certification," Benson-Henry Institute, accessed September 29, 2017. https://www.bensonhenryinstitute.org/training-apply-for-certification/

Chapter 11: Protecting the Movement

1. Margaret Thaler Singer, *Cults in Our Midst: The Continuing Fight Against Their Hidden Menace* (New York: Jossey-Bass, 2003), 209-239.

2. Hari M. Sharma and Deepak Chopra, "Maharishi Ayur-Veda: Modern Insights Into Ancient Medicine," *JAMA* 1991; 265(20): 2633-2637. http://jamanetwork.com/journals/jama/article-abstract/385970

3. Andrew A. Skolnick, "Maharishi Ayur-Veda: guru's marketing scheme promises the world eternal 'perfect health'," Andrew A. Skolnick, posted on October 2, 1991. http://www.aaskolnick.com/mav.htm

4. Ibid.

5. Ibid.

6. Ibid.

7. Corrections. *Newsweek*, November 17, 1997.

8. *Des Moines Register*, November 30, 2011.

9. Home Page, Truth About TM, accessed September 29, 2017.

http://www.truthabouttm.org

10. Letter to TM-EX from Dennis E. Roark. *TM-EX Newsletter* IV(2), Spring 1992. http://minet.org/TM-EX/Spring-92

11. "Commitment of Researchers on the TM Technique to Science," TM Research, Truth About TM, accessed September 29, 2017. http://www.truthabouttm.org/utility/showArticle/?ObjectID=63 5&find=roark&happ=siteAdministrator

12. "DeNaro Affidavit," TranceNet, accessed September 29, 2017. http://minet.org/www.trancenet.net/law/denarot.shtml

13. "Commitment of Researchers on the TM Technique to Science," TM Research, Truth About TM, accessed September 29, 2017. http://www.truthabouttm.org/utility/showArticle/?ObjectID=16 50&find=denaro&happ=siteAdministrator

14. Ibid.

15. Michael A. Persinger, Normand J. Carrey, and Lynn A. Suess, *TM and Cult Mania*, (North Quincy, MA: Christopher Publishing House, 1980).

16. "Does TM Do Any Harm?: Persinger Castillo," Individual Effects, Truth About TM, accessed September 29, 2017. http:// www.truthabouttm.org/utility/showArticle/?ObjectID=834&fin d=persinger&happ=siteAdministrator

17. Home Page, SkepticsOnTM, accessed September 29, 2017. http://skepticsontm.blogspot.com

18. Aviva Berkovich-Ohana et al., "Repetitive speech elicits widespread deactivation in the human cortex: the "Mantra" effect?" *Brain and Behavior* 2015; 5(7), e00346. https://doi. org/10.1002/brb3.346

19. Tom Ball, "Review: Down Joe Kellett's Rabbit Hole," SkepticsOnTM, accessed September 29, 2017. http:// skepticsontm.blogspot.com/2009/03/review-suggestibilityorg. html

20. James Krag, MD, "A Psychiatrist's Perspective: 'Down the TM Rabbit Hole'," SkepticsOnTM, posted on January 14, 2008. http://skepticsontm.blogspot.it/2009/03/psychiatrists-perspective-on-down-tm.html

21. Ibid.
22. "James Krag, M.D. Letter," Truth About TM, accessed September 29, 2017. http://www.truthabouttm.org/utility/show Article/?ObjectID=1839&find=krag&happ=siteAdministrator
23. "Governor Recertification Course: Overview of Policies & Procedures," Wikileaks, accessed September 27, 2017. https://file.wikileaks.org/file/tm-governor-course-2005.pdf
24. Home Page, RelaxationResponse.org, accessed September 29, 2017. http://www.RelaxationResponse.org
25. Alexandra Wolfe, "Transcendental Meditation for Everyone," *Wall Street Journal*, June 30, 2017. https://www.wsj.com/articles/transcendental-meditation-for-everyone-1498842465
26. Email from Marketing and Communications Director, Benson-Henry Institute for Mind Body Care, June 30, 2016.
27. Home Page, RelaxationResponse.org, accessed September 29, 2017. http://www.RelaxationResponse.org
28. "Welcome to the World of TM Blogging!" TM-Free Blog, posted by Michael Doughney on July 30, 2009. http://tmfree.blogspot.com/2009/07/welcome-to-world-of-tm-blogging.html
29. Ibid.
30. Ibid.
31. "Conflicts of interest abound in NYT post on Transcendental Meditation," Health News Review, posted by Joy Victory on June 6, 2016. http://www.healthnewsreview.org/2016/06/conflicts-of-interest-abound-in-nyt-post-on-transcendental-meditation/
32. Norman E. Rosenthal, "Using Meditation to Help Close the Achievement Gap," *Well* (blog), *New York Times*, June 2, 2016. https://well.blogs.nytimes.com/2016/06/02/using-meditation-to-help-close-the-achievement-gap/?_r=0revisitrevisit
33. "Conflicts of interest abound in NYT post on Transcendental Meditation," Health News Review, posted by Joy Victory on June 6, 2016. http://www.healthnewsreview.org/2016/06/conflicts-of-interest-abound-in-nyt-post-on-transcendental-meditation/

34. Shantanu Guha Ray, "Yogi's disciples contort his legacy," *IndiaToday*, June 23, 2012. http://indiatoday.intoday.in/story/maharishi-mahesh-yogi-rs-60000-crore-fortune/1/201925.html

35. "Maharishi Mahesh Yogi," Obituary, *Economist*, February 14, 2008. http://www.economist.com/node/10683705

36. *David Wants to Fly*, directed by David Sieveking (2010; Berlin: Neue Visionen).

37. Robert D. Brook et al., "Beyond Medications and Diet: Alternative Approaches to Lowering Blood Pressure," *Hypertension* 61 (May 2013): 1360-1383. https://doi.org/10.1161/HYP.0b013e318293645f

38. Stephen Propatier, "American Heart Association promotes alternative therapy for hypertension," Skeptoid, posted on May 1, 2013. https://skeptoid.com/blog/2013/05/01/american-heart-association-promotes-alternative-therapy-for-hypertension/

39. https://www.clinicaltrials.gov/ct2/results?term=transcendental+meditation&rank=16#rowId15

40. Tzvi Freeman, "Kosher Meditation: 3 questions to ask before beginning any meditation program," Chabad.org, accessed September 29, 2017. http://www.chabad.org/library/article_cdo/aid/3332306/jewish/Kosher-Meditation.htm

41. Evan Finkelstein, "The Mantras Used In TM Are Some Of The Most Fundamental Vibrations Of Natural Law," On TM Mantras, Truth About TM, accessed September 29, 2017. http://www.truthabouttm.org/truth/IndividualEffects/IsTMaReligion/TMMantras/index.cfm

42. "22 December 2004 Press Conference Highlights," Maharishi's Great Global Events, accessed September 29, 2017. http://press-conference.globalgoodnews.com/archive/december/04-12-22.html

Chapter 12: TM Casualties

1. "Section 2 (Points 10 through 22)," Checking Notes, Meditation Information Network, accessed September 29, 2017. http://

www.minet.org/checking2.html

2. "General Points," Checking Notes, Meditation Information Network, accessed September 29, 2017. http://www.minet.org/checkinggp.html

3. Ibid.

4. Ibid.

5. Larry Husten, "Mysterious Disappearing Paper Finally Reappears In Another Journal," Cardio Brief, November 13, 2012. http://cardiobrief.org/2012/11/13/mysterious-disappearing-paper-finally-reappears-in-another-journal/#comments

6. "Affidavit of Edgar Larry Squires," TranceNet, last modified October 9, 1997. http://minet.org/www.trancenet.net/personal/squires.shtml

7. "DeNaro Affidavit," TranceNet, accessed September 29, 2017. http://minet.org/www.trancenet.net/law/denarot.shtml

8. "Maharishi University of Management stabbing," Wikipedia, last modified August 22, 2017. https://en.wikipedia.org/wiki/Maharishi_University_of_Management_stabbing#cite_note-17

9. Antony Barnett, "Trouble in transcendental paradise as murder rocks the Maharishi University," *Guardian*, May 1, 2004. https://www.theguardian.com/world/2004/may/02/usa.theobserver

10. "Maharishi University of Management stabbing," Wikipedia, last modified August 22, 2017. https://en.wikipedia.org/wiki/Maharishi_University_of_Management_stabbing#cite_note-17

11. Antony Barnett, "Trouble in transcendental paradise as murder rocks the Maharishi University," *Guardian*, May 1, 2004. https://www.theguardian.com/world/2004/may/02/usa.theobserve

12. "TranceNet Personal Histories Archive," TranceNet, last modified October 17, 1997. http://minet.org/www.trancenet.net/personal/index.shtml

13. "Mitchell Kapor on Maharishi, Levitation, and Freedom," TranceNet, last modified February 20, 1997. http://minet.org/www.trancenet.net/personal/kapor.shtml

14. "Marcy's Story," TranceNet, last modified February 20, 1997. http://minet.org/www.trancenet.net/personal/marcy.shtml

15. "German Study," Other Documents, Meditation Information Network, accessed September 29, 2017. http://www.minet.org/Documents/German-Study

16. "The Various Implications Arising from the Practice of Transcendental Meditation," Excerpts & Table of Contents, TranceNet, last modified March 25, 1997. http://minet.org/www.trancenet.net/research/toc.shtml

17. "The Various Implications Arising from the Practice of Transcendental Meditation," Chapter 4 of 7, TranceNet, last modified February 26, 1997. http://minet.org/www.trancenet.net/research/chap4.shtml#4

18. Ibid.

19. Ibid.

20. "The Various Implications Arising from the Practice of Transcendental Meditation," Excerpts & Table of Contents, TranceNet, last modified March 25, 1997. http://minet.org/www.trancenet.net/research/toc.shtml

21. Steven Hassan, *Combating Cult Mind Control: The #1 Best-selling Guide to Protection, Rescue, and Recovery from Destructive Cults* (Newton, MA: Freedom of Mind Press, 2016), 169-172.

22. "Cult or Benign Cure-all? Life in Transcendental Meditation's Hidden Society," a talk by Gina Catena (audio file), TuneIn, 1:16:23. http://tunein.com/embed/player/t89001616/

23. Home Page, Fairfield Cares, accessed September 29, 2017. https://fairfieldcaresct.wixsite.com/website

Acknowledgements

There are many people to thank, all of who played essential roles in making this book possible.

Mike Doughney, Patrick Ryan, Don Krieger, Joe Kellett, and John Knapp had the courage and foresight to create websites providing access to many TM documents. Some websites allowed people to share personal stories about their TM experiences. TM-EX, a newsletter founded by Patrick Ryan in the early 1990s, provided a wealth of information about TM activities worldwide and also functioned as a support group for ex-TM members. Meditation Information Network (minet.org) was created by Mike Doughney and is an archive of TM-EX newsletters and historical TM documents. I believe Mike was the first to provide critical information about TM on the Internet. He is also the coordinator of the TM-Free Blog. Although we've never met, I owe him a tremendous debt of gratitude.

Steven Hassan and Salvador Litvak provided, and continue to provide, invaluable guidance. Gina Catena, Patrick Ryan, Joseph Szimhart, Rabbi Bentzion Kravitz, and Judith Bourque read various drafts of the manuscript and offered well-deserved, critical feedback. One old friendship that was dormant for over ten years was rekindled. This friend challenged me to shift from an academic stance to one that was much more personal and more difficult to write because of the issues he forced me to confront. I thought I had been unscathed by TM. Almost forty years later, I discovered that I wasn't. I believe the book is much better as a result.

I also made a new friend. Early on I made a decision that I wouldn't include any personal stories, even if available online, unless I was given consent. One person I contacted not only allowed me to use his story, but he also made important comments on many drafts of the manuscript. He was a wealth of information on TM, and he opened the door to several important contacts. And moving well beyond the book, we also became friends. We shared information about our families, beliefs, and, despite extraordinarily different lifestyles, found commonality in many areas that are most important to both of us. For different reasons, my old friend and my new friend requested anonymity.

Sara Phillips-Ritchey was a tremendous help with the chapter on TM in public schools.

Tzvi Jacobs and Orly Goldberg were very helpful in identifying and checking some of the research used in the book.

Sally Boyles was my first editor and had the toughest job as my writing skill leaves much to be desired. Not only is she a highly skilled editor, she is also very adept in sifting out unimportant details. Her frequent critiques were delivered so artfully that I rarely felt the knife going in. Kate Rouze did the final editing and, I believe, made the book more readable. She is also a highly accomplished writer and a pleasure to work with. Finally, Melissa Koenig brought her methodical attention to detail, proofreading the entire book, and checking and formatting the references.

CPSIA information can be obtained
at www.ICGtesting.com
Printed in the USA
LVHW022318280822
727054LV00001B/165

9 780999 661505